10/5

D0248920

invisible girl

Mariel Hemingway

Regan Arts.

Regan Arts.

65 Bleecker Street
New York, NY 10012

First Regan Arts hardcover edition, April 2015.

Library of Congress Control Number: 2015930622

ISBN 978-1-941393-24-6

Interior design and illustrations by Alex Camlin
Lettering by Aisling Hickey
Cover design by Richard Ljoenes

Printed in the United States of America

10 9 8 7 6 5 4 3 2 1

contents

To those that could see me . . .
thank you.

introduction

What makes a family sad? It's a hard question to answer. Maybe it's better to think about what makes a family happy and then subtract it. I grew up in a family that had a hard time staying happy. As far back as I can remember, people struggled to be happy, both individually and as a group. Sometimes that meant fighting and angry words. Sometimes it meant hiding from those angry words by withdrawing into the corners of the house. Sometimes it meant turning to other things—other people, other substances. My memories of my family are filled with love, but they're also filled with obstacles and detours that prevented all of us from finding our way to that love. It has taken me decades to see my way around those obstacles but also to see that those obstacles are as much a part of my story as anything else. The child I used to be couldn't possibly understand things the way I understand them now, and that's part of the beauty of remembering: we mark the distance between what we were and what we have become.

1.

no one can see me

I was too early coming into this crazy world, arriving two months before schedule. My mom drank and smoked a lot, and my family liked to joke that I just needed to get some air. I came home just before Christmas after a month in the hospital. I was small, and I guess I took some of the attention away from Margot, my new older sister. It's never good to put an end to your sibling being the focus of your mom and dad's lives. I remember a gray hallway that led to a dressing room/bathroom, and mommy holding me up for Muffet (my new oldest sister) and Margot to see me up close for the first time. One of my scrawny legs fell out of my blanket with a knee that was bigger around than my little noodle legs. Margot glared at me. Her eyes fired up, and I knew from then on that I was in for some trouble.

I'm not sure if a whole day had passed of drinking a few nasty bottles of baby formula—Mommy never let me get too close to her boobs, and I knew then that I was missing something—when Margot found me in the bassinet in Mommy's dressing room. She lifted my limp body, and without much thought and certainly no regret, she dropped me on my head. I would imagine the shock that must have run through me for years, but the scream I let loose was immediate and got everyone's attention. Muffet, Mommy, and Daddy rushed in, and Margot looked surprised and pretended she found me like that. I think the opposite of what Margot had hoped for actually happened. Instead of instant death, I got more cuddles, swaddles, and love, while she was sent to her room with no dinner and no TV. I will hear this story for years, and everyone will laugh at the moment when she lifts me and loosens her grip, but whenever it's retold, I will sneak a glance over at Margot to see how it makes her feel. It seems to upset her in complicated ways: she feels bad for me but also for herself.

Needless to say, I was never left alone again if Margot was in the house. That is when our rivalry began. That is my first memory. I still have a bump on my head to this day.

MY NEXT MEMORIES also take place in that first house, and they come to me mostly in pictures. I remember a front door and going through it. I remember a front hall and shadows on the floor. And I remember that gray corridor that led to the dressing room/bathroom where my mother holds me up so that I can see (and be seen by) the rest of the family. It's winter in Northern California, crisp but not too cold, the mountains in the distance.

Everyone laughs when they see me, but that doesn't mean that everyone is happy. There's Margot, like I said, still reliving the moment when she dropped me. She is seven, buck-toothed, and dark-haired—cute as a girl could be. Muffet is eleven and already a glorious sight: tall, strawberry blond, and elegant. Muffet does things that I can only imagine: she plays tennis and speaks French and knows about all the latest bands. You wouldn't think those things would matter to a baby, and maybe they don't, but they give her a special kind of glow. Muffet is the one who seems to be possessed of grace no matter where she goes or what she does.

Being a baby is pretty easy. I spend my days drinking formula and my nights sleeping or stretched out awake, looking at shadows playing on the ceiling. From early on, I believe that the shadows matter, that they are like clouds in the sky: one second a meaningless pattern of dark and light, the next a secret message being sent only to me.

My next big memory is of my second birthday: November 22, 1963. I am fawned over for days leading up to it. I am dressed like a little baby doll and told how cute I look, and whenever I walk near the kitchen, my mother reminds me that we're going to have a big celebration with all the foods I like. There will be cucumbers, rice, and black beans like my parents made when they lived in Cuba. There will also be a new kind of food called a "cake." Daddy calls me "Marielzy Pumpkin Pudding and Pie," and I wonder if cake is anything like pie, which I already love. My parents talk about this cake constantly: What flavor will it be? What frosting will it have on it? They settle on a recipe by a lady from my parents' wedding picture named Julia Child. My mother went to a fancy French cooking school in Paris with her. Muffet pronounces the name of the cake in what she is quickly told is perfect French. Margot teases me about this cake, telling me that she is going to eat it all before I get any.

The day arrives, the birthday. Am I supposed to feel born? Mommy dresses me in a pretty puffy-sleeved dress with elastic stuff around my chest that makes me feel safe, as if I'm inside a big hug. All morning, I watch Mommy make something special in the kitchen. I think it's the cake because she's acting differently than I've ever seen her before. She has an apron tied around her waist and a smile on her face, and her hands are powdered white. Is that the cake? It seems like magic.

It's also a different kind of day because there's no fighting. Margot is nice to me, and also Mommy and Daddy aren't fighting. Some days they have long arguments when Mommy says Daddy is a slob and fishes too often. Then, when he's gone, she complains that he doesn't make the bed or that he leaves his socks on the floor. He usually doesn't answer. He rolls his eyes at her or goes to the corner of the room and fixes himself a drink. But when he does decide to fight back, he gets loud and mean, and then the house is filled with angry noise. But my birthday has no angry noise, just me and Mommy in the kitchen and the magic cake powder on her hands. I learned early on not to make fusses too often because it makes Mommy angry, and Daddy leaves and Margot and Muffet run away. So I decided that it was my job to always help Mommy be happy by being as happy as possible myself all the time.

And then it all changes. Something happens on the radio, and whatever it is sends my mother to the sink to wash the powder off her hands. Then she carries me to the living room, puts me on the floor, and turns on the television. We watch the little black-and-white screen, where there's a car and a man and a pretty lady wearing a hat. They are smiling and waving from the car, and then the man falls back for some reason, and everyone starts to scream. My father is with us now, and my sisters too, and they're watching the little black-and-white screen more closely than I have ever seen anyone watch anything. People around me say words like "president" and "killed." They try to smile when they realize it's time to eat dinner. There's a different feeling to the day.

After dinner, the lights go off. I'm alone in my chair for a minute. I don't know where everyone has gone. Have they left to go see the man in the car? What is a president, anyway? Some kind of king, I think, which is why everyone is so sad. The king is dead. Finally, I hear a noise behind me. It's my mother's voice. I twist around in my seat to see her walking toward me in the dark, holding something big and dark and round. It smells like sugar and magic powder, and on top of it there are candles flickering. Everyone sings to me, and I get the first piece of cake, which is chocolate with light-brown whipped cream frosting. It's a day I'll always remember for two reasons, and a day everyone else will always remember for one.

NO ONE CALLS ME MARIEL, even though that's my name. I'm Marielzy, and then later Mertle or Mertz. Nicknames are something we give each other in my family. My mom is called Puck, which is not a good name at all. She was nicknamed by the Shoshone Indians who used to come into her father's drugstore when she was little. Puck is supposedly short for *puckinuck*, which means "little one" in Shoshone talk, but when I look it up I can't find it. I hope they weren't just teasing her. I wish Puck weren't what she was called for all the reasons you can imagine. Margot is Mar-gott or Marg. Muffet is called Muffet. Her real name is Joan. And my dad we call Jack, though his name is John Hadley Nicanor Hemingway. Sometimes we call him Dr. Hemingstein or Hemingtrout because he has an encyclopedic knowledge of trout, his favorite fish to catch.

I share a room with Margot, with twin beds, and I keep mine perfectly neat. When I get into bed, I pull the bedspread down just enough to get in without disrupting the tight covers. I want to be invisible, though the truth is that I want to be visible to the fairies that I know are hovering in the room, watching over me. Margot is the opposite. She sleeps wildly, talking to herself and sometimes even walking in her sleep. She makes me nervous. I wish I could share a room with Muffet or my mom, and some nights I do exactly that, slipping out of my bedroom and into theirs. Once I fall asleep on my dad's side of the bed, and in the middle of the night, when it's so dark I can't even see my hand in front of my face, he stretches and accidentally knocks me onto the floor. I lie there stunned, breathing hard. Soon Dad doesn't sleep with Mommy anymore, and I climb in with her some nights and make it to the morning without getting in trouble—unless I move too close to her for a sleepy hug, in which case I get a huge kick in my side that sends me fleeing to the very edge of the bed, motionless. I still sleep on the edge of the bed like that.

Being the youngest means that you're always watching older people, always trying to figure out why they do the things they do. I wonder why Margot yells so much, why she stomps around the house. I guess what I'm trying to let you know is that our house is just uncomfortable. Of

one

course, I don't know any other kind of house, but I feel sad that the only fun comes with a glass of wine or those really weird drinks my parents taught me to make with brown bitter liquid that I poured "two fingers" of over ice.

It's fun to make those drinks but no fun to watch my parents change after they drink them. I don't like how people change after bitter or sour drinks. One minute you feel like things are okay, and the next someone is yelling and someone else is in trouble. My mom and dad are pretty much always unhappy with each other and my sisters. No one is really ever mad at me, which is a good thing, I guess. But sometimes you just kind of wish someone would say something to you other than "finish your dinner" or "take your plate up" or "if you go outside, don't step on any slugs." Who wants to step on slugs?

I also feel like no one can see me. Maybe my invisibility technique at bedtime works too well all the time. I decide that the best thing I can do is to always be helpful. If I'm helpful, then no one will yell at me except Margot, who thinks that if I'm being helpful I'm also a tattletale. I'm not going to lie—I do tattle on her sometimes because she does weird things, and if I tell on her I believe it will bring me closer to my mom. I really love my mom, even

9

though she seems unhappy and angry to everyone but me most of the time. But she is pretty, and she sometimes takes her bony hands and strokes my face—and boy, do I love that. It doesn't happen very often, but you know what it's like to get attention from your mom that's so gentle . . . it just makes me feel dreamy. So that's why I sacrificed Margot, so that I could enjoy a taste of my mother's gentleness. While I am writing this, it doesn't make sense except in my mind.

I'M MOST INTERESTED IN MUFFET. She's a teenager, which means that she gets to go out with friends. She does it all the time—I don't think she likes listening to my parents fight or hearing mean words from Margot. When she comes home, I can see her as she sweeps past the doorway, singing to herself. She has a long velvet jacket that looks black or purple, depending on the light, and tall green kneesocks that cover her knees. You can almost see her underwear because her skirt is really short, which leads to yelling from Mommy. Daddy just sighs and goes on a fishing trip. He loves Muffet. She plays tennis super well. She

wins tournaments, and she is Daddy's favorite person because her tennis is the best he's ever seen and she's smart.
She even speaks French with him, and that was his first
language. Daddy coaches her at tennis and speaks French
with her with a perfect accent (that is important in my
family). He really likes her best of all. I don't think parents
mean to have favorites, but they just do sometimes. It's like
certain kids are everything you want in a best friend, and
you just want to hang out all the time. Mommy favors me,
I think—at least I try to make myself as helpful as a kid
can be for her so that I will be her favorite.

It was pretty clear early on that my coming into the
world was a mistake. I heard Mom and Dad fight about it
once when they thought I was asleep. It's funny how you
find out about things you are scared to know.

MARGOT ISN'T REALLY ANYONE'S FAVORITE. When
I am in bed looking at the shadows on the ceiling, I wonder about that. Who decides how many people are in a
family? A family is a certain shape, and then a new piece
comes along and the shape has to change. If I had never

come along, Margot would be the youngest. Would she be Mommy's favorite then? Maybe Mommy would make cakes for her and she wouldn't feel so angry. And maybe if she wasn't angry, then Muffet would stay at home more, and then maybe Mommy and Daddy wouldn't fight. And if I wasn't there at all, then I wouldn't have to worry about wanting to feel invisible sometimes.

things to think about

1. I was a mistake. I am only here on the earth because my parents got drunk on a fishing trip.

2. Mommy had a baby after Muffet and he was a boy, but he died. They hoped I might be him again.

3. Daddy loves Muffet more than anyone else in the house because she is athletic, smart, and pretty. Mommy feels angry that Muffet gets so much attention.

4. Margot is silly and fun, but she wants too much attention and exhausts everyone.

5. My parents are so unhappy with each other that they don't even sleep in the same room sometimes, though that seems to make them more unhappy.

6. Making yourself invisible is only good when you're trying to avoiding fighting. Otherwise, it's lonely.

2.
my crazy sisters

One night, Muffet comes home really late. I am awake, and I see my bedroom door blow open when the downstairs door slams. I run quickly to the bedroom door and peek out into the hallway. Muffet is walking fast and Daddy is following her, trying to reason with her, but she's not really talking back to him. She's talking out into empty space, saying weird things like she's a butterfly and she's learning to fly, and that the next place she'll be will be a beautiful place without any of the dark colors of the sad world. She's waving her hands as she speaks, and there aren't too many pauses. Daddy calls Mommy, and Mommy yells at Muffet to stop talking nonsense and for that matter to put on some decent clothes. The door to Muffet's room closes. My parents turn, and I run back into bed so they won't see me. A few minutes later, my bedroom door opens. It's Muffet. She stretches out on my bed next to me and talks. Her voice is still that fast voice she was using in the hallway, still without many pauses. She tells me that dreams are magic and fairies are real. She tells me that moving from one place to another is just something that happens in your mind. She tells me all about palaces that you can go to if only you imagine them clearly enough. I fall asleep smiling, but when I wake up she's gone again. Mommy and Daddy are worried. Even Margot is worried.

Life becomes a play, kind of, or at least the people in my life seem like characters. Margot stays mean to me. One day she cuts my eyelashes off while laughing crazily, like someone from *Dark Shadows*. I run to my mom crying, and she strokes my face with her hand. I love that. Another time, Margot and I are at the bus stop waiting to go to school. I am looking for best friend, Chrissy. She doesn't really know she is my best friend, but I want her to be, so I say it to myself whenever I see her. She is beautiful, with a perfect outfit and perfect hair and everything matching everything. My hair is short because my mom cut it in the kitchen with scissors that she keeps with the knives. Is it because she still wants a boy? Chrissy is heading toward the bus stop, and Margot is off to the side swinging a baseball bat. I dash toward Chrissy, and suddenly Margot is right there in front of me, and the bat just explodes into my face. My two front teeth get pushed into the back of my mouth, and I almost choke on them. I don't move. I

can't move. I'm on the ground looking up at the sky, thinking about how the clouds are like the shadows in my room,
when my dad appears, picks me up, and drives me to the
same hospital where I was born. I don't get stitches, but
my whole face looks like a rotten, plump peach and my
lips are swollen for weeks. Again, the episode backfires
for Margot—I get more attention, and she tells me that
I won't get my teeth back for a while.

While Margot and I fight, Muffet continues to disappear. She keeps going out at night and coming back late
talking that fast talk. She says that my parents don't understand the world but that she forgives them. When she
is home, she makes my lunch in the morning. She cuts the
crusts off my mother's homemade white bread and kisses
the top with bright red lipstick so I can see her fairy bless-
ing when I unwrap the sandwich. There's no one as magical as Muffet. And she even knows what to do about my
teeth, or my lack of teeth: she cuts all the hard things,
like apples and cucumbers, into small pieces. Muffet also
brings home food from the city that my mom thinks of as
strange—things like alfalfa sprouts and nut bread. She says
that it's healthy and that my skin will always look beautiful
if I eat it. At the same time, though, she's acting in ways

that don't seem healthy to me. She talks about how rules make no sense and about how even gravity seems like it's just an idea and she's not sure why she has to follow it. Once she says that she is going to take off from our deck and fly into the city lights. She stands on the balcony, her velvet coat floating in the breeze, but before she takes off, Daddy rushes from inside the living room and grabs her and takes her to her room. Mommy and Daddy are constantly yelling at her now—about the city and boys without haircuts and girls without morals. I'm not sure what morals are, but it sounds like it's bad if you don't have them. Once on television, I saw a woman on a game show explaining that her house gets so noisy that she just wants to close her eyes and be taken somewhere far away and magical. Is that what Muffet means?

On nights when everything goes wrong, when Muffet talks fast and Margot says mean things to me and my parents pour too many glasses of whiskey, my dad comes into my room and sits on the bed and cries. He isn't loud about it, but I can hear him. I don't tell him I'm awake because I don't want to embarrass him. I stay silent and still. I don't know what to feel about it other than sad because I know that Daddy just wants to be loved. Being loud after drinking wine doesn't help. Being silent after drinking wine doesn't help. Nothing really gets solved either way.

things to think about

1. You can talk about things that you think you can't—you just have to find a person who's not like the people you're scared to talk to, someone who shows you they're a good person.

2. People you can trust come from school, or they're your friend's parents who seem really kind. They usually want you to talk to a doctor—a doctor who listens.

3. When you decide you need to talk about something it's okay to go blank. You will eventually remember what you need to say.

4. Some doctors are good to talk to—they listen a lot and don't say much, just let you talk and talk, and when you finally open up, they just listen. It feels kind of amazing to be able to let go of stupid stuff. Kind of like writing in a diary, except you know you're being heard.

3.
papa Hemingway

I don't know if I told you, but my grandfather is Ernest Hemingway, one of the greatest writers of all time and in the whole world, I think. He died the same year I was born, only four months before, actually. And when he died, I guess it was kind of like when President Kennedy died—people all over the world were sad. They were particularly sad because he was shot too, like Kennedy, but not by someone else. He shot himself. I was told about this not that long ago, what it means when someone shoots himself. At first, it didn't make sense, but now I am starting to understand that sometimes people's sadness gets so *huge* that they can't feel anything else, and they think that there is nothing else but sadness. It's called depression, and when it happened to my grandfather he got so sad his brain didn't work right, and then he couldn't do the very thing he loved to do, which was write the most amazing books ever.

I think about life being empty, and it doesn't make sense, especially for my grandfather. My dad tells me lots of stories about his dad, and about how Ernest tried to live a life that had everything in it all the time. That meant that he did things like chase bulls down cobblestone streets in Spain. It meant that he hunted big animals in Africa. He believed you had to face the biggest fears of your life. It seems weird to me when people explain it, but I kind of understand. He thought that books would be better if they were inspired by things that made you afraid, that you could show yourself and everyone else that life was at its best when you weren't afraid. That same feeling came to him when he was out on the ocean on his boat, the *Pilar*, which he had in Cuba. He loved the warm weather and loved fishing for the most challenging of fish: the marlin. He based one of his books on it, and that's the first book of his I read in school: it's called *The Old Man and the Sea*.

By the time my grandfather became an old man, though, he wasn't like the old man in the book. He was tired. He drank lots of whiskey like my father and my mother, and it changed him like it changed them. It made him even more tired. He started to lose his ability to write well, and that made him sad, or maybe he just got sad first and then he couldn't write. I'm not sure of the order of things. Even though the entire world loved him, his sadness covered him up like a dark blanket, and he couldn't find his way out. It makes me sad to think about my own father being without a father.

MOM, DAD, MUFFET, MARGOT, and I move from California to Idaho in late 1965 because my dad decides he didn't want to be a stockbroker anymore. He doesn't like wearing a tie and a white shirt. He thinks that in Idaho he can change the way he looks, and by doing that change the way he is. "Everyone get in the car," he says, and we get in the car.

The drive there is fun, except for one major incident. I've had the same blankie since I was born, a soft blue one with satin ribbons along the edges. I'm not sure why it's blue. Maybe my parents wanted a boy or someone got it for them as a present. On the drive up, I am in the front seat, my head in my mom's lap, my feet in my dad's lap. I'm stretched between them, feeling important, protected. I doze off, and when I wake up Mommy and Daddy are fighting. Everyone's face is red, as red as my blanket is blue, and suddenly Daddy grabs my blankie and throws it out the window and onto the dry desert road in the middle of nowhere. I sit up straight to see it flutter once, and then it's gone. Mommy screams for him to stop and get it, and he raises his hand and says that if anyone says another word he may hit someone. I don't think he will, but you never know when someone's face is that red. I fold myself up into a tiny ball, scared and skinny, and start praying that he will stop and turn around. Mommy strokes my face, and I cry silently. Even Margot feels bad for me, which is one of the ways I know that I'm really upset.

Arriving in Idaho with no blankie is a blur. We get set up in the new house, but sleeping is different, terrible. I can't really do it. Mommy spends her days on the phone calling back to California, trying to get a new blanket, or convince someone to retrieve my old one from the highway. Then one day Mommy comes to me with a smile. She has my blanket—or rather, a brand new one, which is even better. But it smells wrong. I frown and shake my head. Mommy washes it and hangs it on the line, and when it dries, the magic comes back. It has the right texture and smells a little like the wind, which is just right, and Mommy is sure to wash it over and over again to try to tatter the edges a little just like the old one.

In our new home, Daddy gets his way by starting a new

three

life as a fish and game commissioner. He looks after wild-
life and helps make rules to protect them. He's not against
hunting, but he thinks there have to be rules for when and
where you can do it. Lots of his attention goes into fishing.
He loves fly-fishing, which is fishing with fake bugs that
he makes in our basement with threads and feathers, like
little sculptures. When a fish gets on your line in a catch-
and-release zone, you have to put it back into the water.

Daddy shares nature with me. He takes me into the
wilderness lots of days, shows me how nature is always
kind and smart. He tells me that nature doesn't ever make
you feel bad about yourself. It always wants you to just
breathe it in and love it. He tells me that nature is close to
what our pure hearts were like before the stuff that happens inside the house makes you feel bad. Nature is always
forgiving and lets you have chance after chance to feel
good about your life and make happy choices. I've decided
that nature is my friend, my very best friend, and from
what I can understand about God, it's where He lives. And
that is about the most amazing thing to think about ever.
I spend hours outside thinking about how everything in
nature is full of good and kindness and love. It never dis-
appoints me.

DADDY TAKES ME FISHING and hunting and hiking lots of days. We walk the mountains or hills for hours looking at different birds and wading in rivers. He tells me about currents and how to read the river, about how to tell what kind of food the fish are eating by what bugs you see flying around and the number of rings you see on top of the water, or something like that. Some of those details I don't pay close attention to, but I love being there. I'm not too good at fishing, but I can cast my line, and my dad likes that. Most of the time I dangle my feet over a tube into the river or wade in the current looking at the colorful rocks beneath the water. I like watching bugs land on my knees and the hawks when they circle the sky looking for a groundhog or mouse. Daddy says that the hawks circle their prey for a while before they make a swoop to get lunch. Then, after that, the crows circle and eat up what the hawks leave behind. It's all part of a circle of life, and if we hunt in the right places at the right times, then we become a part of the circle too. Still, it doesn't make a whole lot of sense because we have such

three

an advantage over them with guns. But the quiet time outside always feels okay.

WE HUNT IN THE FALL—chukars, doves, and ducks—and we store them in a huge freezer. Daddy never shoots deer or elk because no one at home will let him. He tries once, but I cry and beg for Bambi's life, and even Margot and Muffet say they'll never talk to him again if he puts a bullet in a deer. I'm not sure it makes sense. Why is a deer worth protecting but not a bird? But I go along with it anyway. When we do go bird hunting, some birds get super scared and play dead, and our dog Elsa brings them back to us unhurt. Those birds come with us. I build a huge outdoor cage and "nurse them back to health." I even wear a homemade nurse cap. A couple of times I am able to make them better, but a couple of times our cat gets in the cage.

DO YOU EVER FEEL like where you are is the center of the whole world? That if you think about something really hard, you can make it happen—but you know that you have to wish and pray and think about it all the time for it to work? There are times, living in Ketchum, Idaho, when I begin to think that if I really focus on something, I can make it happen.

things to think about

1. The outdoors feel like where God lives, and He shows Himself by showing you all kinds of cool stuff: nests with eggs, baby birds (actually all birds), and butterflies— especially when they come super close to your face.

2. If you can be as still as a rock for a long time, then hummingbirds, butterflies, and squirrels will eventually think you're one of them.

3. No one can make you feel stupid when you're outside in nature by yourself.

4. You are powerful when you are still and quiet.

5. Forests are good for screaming and getting angry because they never get mad back at you. Plus, it makes you feel better for a while.

6. Jumping into cold water makes you feel more awake than when you sip your mom's coffee.

7. Fairies are real. They might be in your room, but they are definitely in the forest. Hummingbirds may actually be fairies, just so you know.

4.
invisible girl

By the time we move to Ketchum, I'm already done with kindergarten. For some reason, though, the Ketchum school wants me to repeat it. I don't want to go. I feel ugly: short hair, missing teeth, too tall. Ugh. There's a school picture of me with other the kids in my class, and I look like a weird, giant boy hulking in the background. I'm wearing a striped green and white shirt that makes my face look wider than normal, if that's possible, and pants that ride too high above my ankles, though not intentionally. I didn't know about it being a picture day and made a seriously poor fashion choice—not that I had many choices anyway. I look like a boy, while the girls I long to know are small, wear girly clothes, and are already friends with one another. They're the ones who always sit in the front row.

Rather than suffer through a year of looking weird, I ask Daddy if I can learn to ski instead of going to school. I promise to go to the mountain every single day and get really good at it, and I promise to get really good grades when I go back to first grade the next year. He agrees, which shocks me. Is he joking? But the next week I have a season pass with my photo on it, all gums and pudgy cheeks. I have privileges to use the mountain every day from 8:30 in the morning until it closes. I have a bunch of lessons with Mrs. Sherntanner, who has a new baby and lots of older kids, and who is nicer to me than anyone I've ever met. And last but not least, I have a number to remember. It's called a J number, and it's a charge account number so I can get all the food I want from the Sun Valley cafeteria. I am so proud of my J number. I repeat it to myself all the time, under my breath.

The mountain opens on Thanksgiving Day, and Dad drives our wood-paneled station wagon to the hill. Each day starts with tiny marshmallows in my hot chocolate and big boots that get laced up tight. Tight means safe, just like with my bedsheets. It's like being hugged from the outside.

When I start skiing it is slow going. I make a pizza pie with my skis to control my speed, and that doesn't always go well. But after just a few days I get better, and before long my afternoons are all about going up the chairlift and down the mountain by myself. By December, I am friends with all the staff and the teachers and the hot chocolate makers. They even throw in extra marshmallows and give me special bags of potato chips at lunch.

Since everyone is older, I bring my best friend with me. That's my Skipper doll, who's named Skippy. (What else would you name a Skipper doll?) I like Barbie, but her weird, bumpy boobs bother me, and also Barbie isn't brave enough to go up the mountain. I bundle up Skippy in wool pants and a tiny sweater from my godmother, who is magical because she can make Barbie clothes that look like my very own. Skippy stays warm inside my jacket sleeve. On the way up the mountain, I talk to her nonstop. We discuss the fastest route down. We laugh at the big gap in my mouth and how my hat doesn't match my outfit.

As I get better, I also get more courageous, and I decide that Skippy needs more action in the snow. Out of the blue, I throw her out into the frozen mounds of new snow, screaming that I'll be there in a second to save her life. Rushing off the lift and tucking like a racer, I go straight down to her side again and again. I rescue her so many times, and each time she's relieved, an expression of joy on that beautiful unchanging face of hers. Once I throw her too far, and I jump right off the lift so that she won't be buried under the snow. It sounds more dramatic than it is. That year there is so much snow that jumping off the lift is almost like hopping to the ground.

Other kids don't know about Skippy. If they did, maybe they'd be nicer. An older girl on the ski team comes by, and I realize that it would be nice to ski with a friend, so I start talking to her. She dares me to stick my tongue to the post of the chairlift, which I do, only to realize a second later that there's nothing fun about having your tongue attached to frozen metal. The chairlift guy stops the whole lift and pours warm water on my tongue. I am happy to feel it there again. With tears streaming down my face, I take Skippy into the lodge and we help clean the tables for the rest of the afternoon. From that moment on, I decide not to talk to or try to make friends with kids from the Valley. But it is still the best year of school I've ever had, even if it's only ski school.

The frozen pole incident is one of many that makes me realize I don't like being around other kids. Do I act in a way that makes them not like having me around? Is it because of how I look? I try to look nice, but with my short hair, skinny legs, wide face, and missing front teeth, it isn't easy. Is it because I laugh too much? I do laugh all the time. I know I'm doing it, but I can't stop. Inside, I don't feel dumb. But when I open my mouth, I can't think of anything to say—certainly nothing that expresses my thoughts—and so I giggle a high-pitched giggle that annoys everyone, especially me.

THE YEAR AFTER SKI SCHOOL, it's back to regular school, where I still feel awkward about how I look and the way I giggle all the time seems to be getting worse. It's also strange because I'm going to Ernest Hemingway Grade School. Does that sound cool, to go to a school with the same name as yours? It's not, at least not completely. I'm excited the first day because I have new dresses and longer hair. I look like a girl, and that's what I tell myself going through the halls of the school. It smells like new carpet and paint, and there is a lot of plastic blowing around where men are still working on making new walls. The desks face each other in pairs, and I sit opposite Chip Atkinson, a cute boy whose parents own the grocery store. Down the way from us there's Marcella, Lisa, Lance, Sean, and a few others.

First and second grade aren't horrible, and I manage

to get through them without much of an issue. But I am getting shier by the day. There is a big school event every Friday when we all sit together and sing and share, and I actually pray that I'll get sick so that I can go home. At the same time, I *love* to sing. I sing in a voice so high it hurts my own ears, though. At least I'm in tune—or at least I think I am. My mother can't sing at all. When we go to church, which is only twice a year, she sings super loud and it is *horrible*. I know I'm better than she is.

It seems like all the other kids have recess, homework, singing, clothes, their hair, and sports figured out. It's as though all the kids I watch in school or on the playground are born knowing which sports they're great at and never once have to figure it out. I am the kid who gets picked not last but second to last—and not even in a hateful way, but as if it doesn't matter to anyone. I almost wish the other kids would notice me more, but I'm not sure I could handle it.

MY TEACHER, MRS. BUTTERFIELD, makes everyone stand and look to the corner flag for the Pledge of Allegiance. Everyone knows it except me, so I lip-sync with *four*

anyone I can see out of the corner of my eye. When I sit back down, Chip looks strange. He has a troubled look on his face, and he goes pale and coughs. Then, all of a sudden, everything he ate for breakfast is all over my desk. I start to panic. Mrs. Butterfield tells someone to take Chip to the bathroom while she takes me the girls' room, where she tries to wash me off. I burst into tears, wanting my mom, wanting to go home. When we get back to the classroom, the janitor has poured banana-scented powder around the desk.

The picture of Chip throwing up stays with me, and I become obsessed with the idea of vomiting—or rather *not* vomiting. I constantly think about how to avoid it, about what will happen if I do. I take stomach medicine, antacids, and Pepto-Bismol that I steal from my parents' medicine cabinet. It's wrong to steal, and I know that, but my fear is overwhelming. Once or twice I even take medicine from the drugstore without paying.

✳ ✳ ✳

ONE AFTERNOON AT SCHOOL, we do the President's Physical Fitness Test. It's a big deal, and if you do well, you get a note from the president. You have to climb a rope, do push-ups and sit-ups, and run as fast as you can across the gym floor. I do everything but the rope climb. I am one of two kids who can't finish. The cool kids, and even the ones who aren't cool, get to the top of the rope so quickly. I only get three feet off the ground before I start thinking about how my feet are supposed to hold the rope with my toes. That's when I let go. When I hit the ground, everyone is already heading out of the gym for homeroom. I sit there for a minute and try to imagine myself doing it again, my feet wrapped around the rope. I see myself at the top. I wait until the gym is empty and try it again, and this time I make it to the top. Now I'm even more confused, wondering why I can do things alone that I can't do in front of other people.

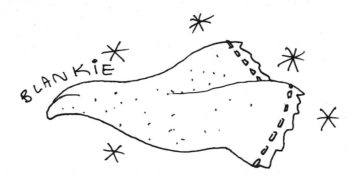

things to think about

1. Why am I one person in the outside world and another in my head? Does everyone feel that way?

2. Why is it sometimes easier to be around adults?

3. If I didn't show up every day for the school bus, would it come at all? Would school happen at all? It sounds selfish, but I bet everyone wonders about it.

4. Can teachers hear your thoughts?

5. Will Margot be my babysitter when my parents go out to dinner? Does she have to be?

6. Is my blankie magic? I think so.

5.
mine time

I meet my first best friend, Ceilee, the summer after second grade. She lives off Highway 93, which is famous for going from the North Pole down through California to Mexico. I bike to Ceilee's house every day in the summer, and we play with dolls and make forts and build houses for animals, both real and stuffed. She has a normal family, which is sort of like mine except that everyone does things together like take trips to museums and historical sites or have picnics. When they sit down to eat, everyone prays and laughs. At our house, there aren't many picnics and there isn't much laughing. Daddy gets up before dawn and goes out fishing. No one sees him for a while. Mommy gets up a little later. She's in a bad mood until her coffee kicks in, and then she's only in a slightly better mood. When she says nice or kind things, I remember them because they're not very common. Ceilee doesn't come to my house very often, and I see why.

The one thing that is strange about Ceilee's house is the kind of food they eat: SpaghettiOs and Rice-A-Roni, foods that would make my dad shake his head if he saw them. For me, it's a kind of amusement park. I try Cap'n Crunch, which I love, and I try to convince Mommy that we need a box of our own. I also like Lucky Charms, which has all these marshmallow shapes floating in the milk, though I don't like those as much—they're more fun to look at than they are to eat.

Right around that time, something happens to Daddy on one of his hikes. It's an early morning hike, and he doesn't take any kids along or even my mom—he's by himself, except for our new yellow lab, Elsa. When he comes home that night, he says that he feels awful. He's more tired than usual, and he has an ache in his chest. Mommy thinks she knows why. It's because he eats too much and drinks too much. She's always telling him about his eating and drinking, and she tells him again. But this time she's wrong. After ten minutes, his chest hurts even more. He is starting to feel like he might throw up, and his arm is numb. "I think maybe I'm dying," he says, but not in a loud voice or a funny voice. Now Mommy looks scared. She gets him to the car, and we rush to the hospital. The doctor, who sometimes fishes with Daddy and definitely drinks cocktails with him, says he is having a heart attack.

five

He tells my mother something in a soft voice, and then turns to me. "A heart attack means his heart is working too hard," he says. "We need to keep him here to make sure we give it some help for a while." We leave Daddy there attached to wires and boxes that beep and whir, and he's there for weeks. We can only visit him for a few minutes every day, and in fact I am not supposed to be there at all because I am too young. But the nurses like me and sneak me in. Daddy looks smaller at times, quieter than I remember. I'm not scared that he'll die. I don't think that's possible. But I wonder how things will change.

Soon, my wonder has answers. When Daddy comes home from the hospital, there are several major changes. It seems easier to put them in a list because that's how I hear them, over and over again.

NO MORE SMOKING. Daddy has to quit, so Mommy does too. She smokes in secret in the laundry room with the door closed and thinks no one notices. But billows of smoke come out when she opens the door. "What?" she demands. "Get your tush outta here." She swats me, and I don't dare say a word about it.

NO MORE ALCOHOL. Well, besides wine. Wine is healthy for you, but only if you drink a tiny bit. Not bottles like everyone used to drink.

NO MORE QUESTIONING. Daddy used to be quiet, but since his heart attack he says he's not going to be walked on anymore, and everyone has to pay attention to him and behave or he could die. He is the king of his castle, which is our house.

NO MORE STRESS. This is rule number four, but in a way it's rule number one because it's the most important of them all. Daddy needs quiet. No one can raise her voice or get mad. Stress makes things worse. "Be nice!" Daddy yells.

A heart attack gives you the right to do whatever you want. Nobody can tell you what to do anymore. It's a way of getting attention. It gets you lots of things, in fact. One thing that Mommy and Daddy talk about also happened when the heart attack happened, and that's that the pretty nurse in the hospital paid too much attention to Daddy. Mommy didn't like that. It upset her as much as the heart attack, maybe even more, but she can't say anything about it. No more stress. That's rule number four.

Oh! Wine Time: that's this weird thing my parents come up with after Daddy's heart attack. It starts anytime after five o'clock, give or take an hour on the before side. Everyone is convinced that drinking red wine will keep them healthy and happy. *Not so fast, family!* I notice no difference between their usual drinking and Wine Time. Here's how it goes: There's a huge bottle of wine, and everyone gets a glass except me—I think it's gross. They add a couple of ice cubes, and *voila*—as my dad would say in French—a lovely watered-down glass of wine. But after four or five big glasses, no one is acting lovely. One glass, and they are funny and nice; two glasses, and they start getting snippy; three glasses, and a fight breaks out about food or politics or Mommy not getting enough money for supplies from Dad. (She gets an allowance like a kid, and it's never enough.) Of course, then they need a fourth and fifth glass because they got so mad during the third glass. I call them "the angry glasses," and after that no one says a word anymore—there's just a lot of sighing and huffing. Usually after Wine Time and dinner, Margot heads into town to the Pioneer Saloon for more drinks with her friends. She's eighteen now, so she can do what she wants, and she does. Muffet has gone to Paris, so it's just the four of us.

I GUESS NOW is as good a time as any to tell you about Muffet. Remember when I told you about her talking about being magical and wearing her fairy clothes? That was in California, and in Idaho she's still doing it.

One night, Mommy wakes me up. "Let's go," Daddy says. We're in the car, but I'm still not totally awake. I watch the stars out the window as we drive into Ketchum. In town, Mommy rolls down her window and Daddy does the same, and both of them yell Muffet's name into the dark streets. "Muffet?" I ask. I don't understand. She's not in the car with us.

Then we see her, running down Sun Valley's main street, completely naked. She's laughing, singing, leaping like a ballerina. There's a scarf in her hands stretched out along the length of her arms like wings. Daddy gets her into the car, which isn't easy—Muffet seems possessed by something that maybe isn't entirely human. At home, she sleeps, finally, and the next day a doctor comes and gives her a shot that keeps her in bed, mostly sleeping, for two more days. When she wakes up, Mommy and Daddy have a long talk with her about drugs, which are pills that older kids swallow to make the world either more or less interesting. If you're not careful with drugs, they can really hurt you. Muffet wasn't careful. Everyone decides that the only thing that's going to stop Muffet from taking drugs and running in the street again is to go to a special school up north.

It's sad around the house without Muffet. Margot is bossier than ever. She doesn't let me into the bathroom, doesn't let me brush my hair or use the curlers, doesn't let me open the refrigerator for milk. I want Muffet to come back. I ask my parents when she's coming back from school. Then one day we go to visit her, and that's when I find out that her school isn't really a school at all. It's a big building with iron bars on the windows, and it's filled with people who can't control how they act or feel. Some people say the word "mental." Some people say the word "facility." I try not to say any words. I just think about Muffet inside there. We wait about an hour, and she comes out. She's wearing high moccasins and a short leather skirt, with her hair in braids. Everything she has is beaded—bracelets from art class, braids with leather ties. She looks just like Sacagawea, who I learned about in school.

We visit Muffet a few more times, and finally Mommy and Daddy tell me she's ready to come home. The only thing that's strange is that her skin is yellow, and we have to wait in the little town of Blackfoot for two days while the yellowness goes away. It's from drugs, the yellowness—not the kind of drugs that put her there in the first place but good drugs that will keep her safe when she's out. I don't completely understand why certain drugs are good and others are bad. How do you know which pills will hurt you and which will help? It doesn't make sense to me, and it doesn't seem to make sense to Muffet either. When she finally gets home, she spits them out. I don't tell anyone because I don't want her to get into trouble. The first night Muffet's home, I lie awake looking at the shadows on the ceiling. There's a shape that looks sort of like a tree. Does that mean that the family is about to grow again? That it's a new season? Maybe Daddy's recovery from his heart attack and Muffet's time at the hospital are over. Maybe we're heading toward an easier time.

things to think about

1. Some drugs, like the ones Muffet took, take you away
    from normal. They made her feel like she could see the
    whole earth and all the stars at one time. They gave
    her a crazy brain that could never be normal again. At
    least it seems that way.

2. Drugs that are supposed to help you feel normal make
    some people, like Muffet, feel bad. She says they make
    her feel sad and tired, and she definitely can't see fairies
    anymore. Are there other ways to make her normal?

3. I don't ever want to take drugs. I just go outside. I walk
    to the tops of mountains. I never feel lonely or scared
    there. I look at faraway things and big things made
    small, and all my worry goes away. That feels normal.
    I wish Muffet could do this.

6.
first kiss

Mrs. Wilde, my third-grade teacher, has pretty black hair done in a shape that makes it look like a bonnet. I like her so much that I like doing well in her class, to the point where I shed some of my shyness and even start to read in front of everyone. That means that I have more friends, which means more hopscotch and jump rope and cat's cradle with Kelly and Lisa and other girls. We make cootie catchers, those folded paper things that have numbers and messages inside, and when you open them up they tell you to pinch a boy or laugh out loud in class for no reason. I play tag with other kids and scream happily when I can't quite catch Lance. I trade lunch with Katrin, who never has sandwiches but brings chicken legs or round cheese in red wax with big hunks of salami. I still play with Ceilee, but she's more of a summer friend.

One day in third grade, a bunch of girls stand outside and wait for a bunch of boys to come out to the playground. We've made a pact, which is that we will kiss and be kissed. It's time. The kids in Hailey, the next town over, do it all the time, and we don't want to be left behind. I want to be paired with Sean because he's the boy I think about most of the time. I like the way he smiles at me, and I like the way I feel when I say nice things about him. I think that I might be in love with Sean and wonder if he's in love with me. But Sean's not included in the kissing event. Instead, I am paired with Lance. Lance is nice too, though not as nice as Sean, and he's short, which means that the kiss is kind of complicated. I tell him to stand on the big snowdrift next to me so he can reach. On the count of three, Lance and I lock lips. Our mouths mush together. After about ten seconds, I look over at Kelly, who is kissing Mark, but she's not looking at me, and I close my eyes. I don't know if I'm supposed to breathe or suck in all the air or put my hand on Lance's neck or make a fist or what. The kiss goes on and on. Finally we separate, and there's a pop like a soda bottle when you open it. For a few weeks, we're legendary, the kids who kissed for three minutes. We are record-holders. But Lance and I never kiss again.

six

EVERY FRIDAY AND SATURDAY night at the Sun Valley Opera House, there is an evening movie. It's the best part of the week, by far. The whole town—or at least the whole town of kids—is there, with popcorn, Milk Duds, Jolly Ranchers, and soda. I usually have only Swedish Fish because they don't make me sick.

In winter, I take my dog Elsa down to the movies. I'll do what kids always do at the Sun Valley Opera House, which is run up the aisle, talk to other kids, scramble back to my chair. You might miss some of the movie, but no one's watching anyway. And my plan is to sit with Sean. I don't think we'll kiss, but I have a secret plan, which is to hold hands with him.

The movie is going to start in just a few minutes. Sean hasn't arrived yet. I can feel my heart in my neck, like a rabbit's legs thumping. I start to giggle. What will he do? Will he say anything to me? Will he sit and not move? Will he have a soda? If he does, what kind will it be? And while he is drinking it, how will we hold hands? The previews start, and I think maybe he won't come at all. Maybe he's changed his mind. Maybe he's sitting with a group of boys someplace else in the theater, looking over at me. Mark, who is Sean's brother, is sitting with Kelly, his kissing partner.

On the screen is a preview for the movie that's coming next week, which is *Chitty Chitty Bang Bang*. It looks great. The car flies! But where's Sean? What happened to him? Mark whispers something to Kelly, who whispers something to me: Sean has chores at home and is running late. "No problem," I say, half watching the movie, trying to smile. I see a kid out of the corner of my eye and I squeak, thinking it might be Sean, but it's another kid asking if he can sit in the empty seat next to me. Kelly shakes her head. "It's taken," she says. More time goes by, another ten minutes, and I start to give up. Then I see Sean with his white-blond hair making his way across the theater. He sits down right next to me. I look over at him and giggle. I try to say hi, but it comes out so softly that I can't even hear myself speak. "What?" he says, wrinkling up his face. "Nothing," I say. "Just saying hi." Sean has no soda. I need to pee, but no way am I losing my spot next to him.

Sean and I watch the movie, but he looks so cute that I decide I want to watch him instead of the movie. His hair goes every which way, and his face is really white, but his cheeks are pink from skiing all afternoon. Sean is on the junior A team—I am on the B team—and he is good. He is the funniest boy on the team. He makes jokes, and everyone laughs. He must be nice to have as a brother, which is all he has—no sisters, just three brothers. Kelly tells me that he and his brothers have to take care of themselves some afternoons because their mom works long hours as a nurse and their dad lives somewhere else. The boys do all of the cooking and cleaning.

The movie is still playing, and I still have to pee. I look back at the clock, and thirty minutes have gone by with no hand-holding at all. I move my hand to the edge of my right leg to give it a chance of being taken, and then I move it to the chair arm. What's it doing there? But it works. He takes my hand and scoots up in his seat, and so do I. Now the arm of the chair is not in the way, and part of my hand is touching his leg. If my heart was in my throat before, now my whole body is thumping. Nothing could be more amazing than this feeling. There is total happiness in my hand, and when he interlaces our fingers together, it's pure heaven.

We never look at each other, but when the movie ends he looks at me and says he is sorry he was late, but if I want we can go play on the preschool swings near the post office. I say sure and smile again as he takes off in a run after Andy Lund, who has come by to hit him on the arm.

"I'll be a sec," I call after him, and I hurry to the bathroom. The line is endless. I don't wash my hands because I don't want to wash off the memory.

When I come outside, fifteen minutes have gone by, and Sean has already gone to the post office. When I get there, out of breath, he is gone, and Kelly is waiting next to her dad's car to make sure my dad is coming. "I can't believe he left," I say, and Kelly tells me not to worry. "He likes you," she says. I tell Kelly that she can leave, that my dad will be along any second. There are still a couple of kids running around the post office, but most everyone has been picked up, and there's no one at the swing sets. Car lights keep coming . . . one, two, and three more. Each one might be my dad but isn't. Sitting on the edge of a parking space, I wait while watching the sky get darker and the stars get brighter. The sky is always pretty and mysterious, and I wonder what is beyond the stars. I am not scared, even though I am by myself. I hear footsteps, which is scary, but it is only the security guard for the Sun Valley hotels, and I know him. "Are you okay, Mariel?" "Yeah, sure," I answer, my daddy is coming. We live way out of town. He probably thought the movie was longer." Lots of movie nights Daddy is late picking me up, especially on Friday or Saturday nights, when my parents have people over for dinner and they drink lots of wine.

MY DAD LOVES WINE. Big deal wine . . . wines that have names as long as the alphabet . . . ones that need to be stored in the basement and put on their side . . . wines that needs to "breathe," which means sit open on the fancy table my mother has me help her set in the dining room for guests for an hour or two before people come over. I know how to open a bottle of wine by myself even at age nine. I pour and twist and wipe it with a napkin like I work in a fancy restaurant. I never make a drip ever, and I get a lot of praise for it. I even know how to serve to the right and clear from the left. I know when to serve the salad and where to place it and how many forks must be on the table (let's just say it's a lot, and they start out small and get bigger as they get closer to the plate). My mother says that if you learn all this stuff and the good manners that go along with it—no elbows on the table, chew with your mouth closed, no cussing, and stick your pinkie out when you drink from a wine glass or teacup—then you can eat with the queen. I don't care much about the queen, especially since she is all the way in England, but okay. I kind

57

of like all the rules that go with eating fancy dinners. I like how everything is clean and in order before the party begins, and I like watching Daddy and Mommy get ready, how they're so excited to share their food and wine and my dad's encyclopedic knowledge with their fancy friends. I like the parties at the beginning because when other people are around, everyone gets along. It really isn't until the party is over that everything gets uncomfortable—sometimes worse.

Sean doesn't abandon me after the post office. We talk on Monday at school. We go to the swings by the post office, and he holds my hand again. But then, my worst fear comes true. He moves to Pocatello to be with his dad. "I don't know when I'll be moving back," he says. "I'll come back for summers." Summer is so far away. It's in another year. Eventually, I wash my hand.

things to think about

1. When you are left in the dark by yourself and get a little scared, you will be okay if you look for the biggest, brightest stars.

2. Holding hands is the best thing in the world, way better than kissing someone you don't like.

3. Only kiss or hold hands with someone you like a lot.

4. Only like someone a lot who likes you back. How do you know? He likes you if he takes your hand and interlaces his fingers with yours. He likes you if he gets hit with something and has to go after the mean guy who did it to defend your honor. He likes you when you catch him looking at you, even though you were doing the same thing.

5. You like him if all you can feel for days after you hold his hand is a strange ache in the space between your fingers.

6. Your parents sometimes can't teach you about love because no one taught them about it.

7.
the sun will come out

I love summer—not just because school is out, but because I am. You get to be outside all day, every day. I like being outside because it's not inside, where the fighting is, but also because outside means rocks and streams and woods. From the time I can ride a bike, I ride into town by myself. I go to Ketchum after breakfast, which is a fun ride because it's a little bit downhill and makes me feel strong. In town there's tons to do. I can hang out by the river below my grandfather's house. I can eat at Atkinsons' Market or take my lunch to the river. I can watch the geese and ducks swim in the pond and feed them the crusts of my sandwich or crumbs from my potato chip bags. Sometimes I use my J account to buy things other than food: Juicy Fruit gum or Hostess Fruit Pies. At least once a week, I buy some stomach medicine, TUMS or Pepto-Bismol, to prevent any sickness. I try to keep those off the J account, though, because there's a record of what I buy, and that can mean big trouble. Margot has already been caught charging grown-up drinks like beer.

Bike riding is only part of the summer. Lots of days I swim in the lake, which isn't nearly as cold as it is during winter but is still cold enough to be an alarm clock for your insides. It wakes you up fast. Other days I climb the rock near the lake. It's a place for climbers to practice on after they come from the Elephant's Perch, the sporting goods store in town. Kids climb without ropes, though tourist kids only go up the easy side. We climb the hard side, and whoever gets to the top first is king or queen. I teach my new puppy, Mr. Bubba, to climb the easy side with me for hugs. Other times my friends and I do ding dong ditch, which is when you run up to a condo or hotel room, ring the bell, and run away as fast as you can. Even though we sometimes get caught, the people from the resort don't seem to mind. We giggle so much that it's hard to treat us like criminals. At home, we have a trampoline, so I can jump and jump and jump. I think summer and sunshine on your face all day is total happiness: bikes and games and swimming and dogs and friends. As far as I'm concerned, there are not enough summer hours to do all I want to do.

And then, it gets even better. At the end of each summer I go to Oregon to stay with Mary Kay and Dan, my godparents, who live on a farm with no kids and lots of animals. I spend time with them and learn to sew, feed chickens, and pick baskets full of vegetables out of Mary Kay's garden. There are times when I wish I was their real daughter because I get so much attention. They have an attic filled with dolls and dollhouses, toys and baby clothes—all handmade. I get to choose which room I stay in, either the cubbyhole attic with the toys or the one close to Mary Kay's. Every year, Mary Kay brings me to the fair, and we enter some of the competitions. Since she always wins ribbons, it makes me feel like I've won them too. I love Dan and Mary Kay. And they love me with all the loving they have stored up for the babies they can't have. It's so easy to be with them. And they don't drink, so no one ever changes. I get to be me, whether it's in the orchard or the attic or on the porch swing. It is the only time I ever remember when I don't have to worry about taking care of something at home: cleaning, carrying, worrying. It's a vacation just for me: no Muffet, no Margot, not even Mom or Dad. I am the center of the world there.

things to think about

1. *Happiness is summer.*

2. *Summer is happiness.*

3. *Cold water makes everything better. It's as if you can feel the world inside you.*

4. *If you have a long bike ride home, jump into a river before you go. By the time you're home, your clothes are dry and you aren't overheated.*

5. *Being outside in the summer never gets boring, even when you're by yourself.*

6. *If you push yourself really hard at climbing or biking, you'll feel confidence in yourself.*

8.
winter chill

As beautiful and happy as things are outdoors, that's how sad and dark they can be indoors. Whenever my parents have a dinner party, they start the night happy. There's hearty laughter and hugs and people saying interesting things to each other. By midnight, though, when the guests leave, there's yelling and fighting. I try to sleep, but the noises keep me awake. The fighting only stops when Mommy comes upstairs by herself and Daddy goes to his room in the basement. Some nights, Mommy lets me rest in her bed while she cries and talks about her sad life with Daddy.

When she falls asleep, I go downstairs to clean. It's easier to clean at night by yourself. No one complains. The only noises are the water running in the sink, the clinking of empty wineglasses and dishes, and the whooshing of drinks being poured down the drain. None of it smells very good: the wine, the cheese, and the drinks all mix together to make a sour, sad odor. Our cat, Kitsy, watches me from the little box where she eats on top of the food warmer. It feels like she's helping me, even though she just watches me. I gather all the dishes from the dining room and rinse everything well, load the dishwasher the way Mommy showed me, put the knives and forks and spoons in their own special slots. I have to wash and dry the good crystal glasses by hand and put them away. It takes me an hour to clean the dining room and kitchen.

I make sure the broken glass is swept up—it'd be nice to be able to vacuum, but then everyone would wake up and get angry, so I sweep and sweep until I see no more sparkling on the floor. I have to be careful because I don't wear slippers, and I don't want to cut my feet. My goal is to have everything perfect by morning. Then no one will remember that they fought and no one will have to talk about it and it will be a happy day. Sometimes it works, and sometimes I have to stay and help pull weeds in the garden before I can get on my bike and go to town.

SOME DAYS I'M TIRED of school. Our teacher is Ms. Haire, and the "Ms." means she's not married. My mommy says she's a woman's libber, which doesn't sound nice when she says it. But Ms. Haire has a soft voice and never screams at kids. Skiing is easier too. I am better on the mountain, and my dad even lets me ski race. It's so much pressure. Every girl is so focused on winning, and they look at each other before the race and scowl to let the other girls know that they don't have a chance. It doesn't seem much fun, and I have to use my stomach medicine a lot.

One day, I have an embarrassing accident. After school, the team is practicing gates on Dollar Mountain. I have to pee. But since I never push to the front of the line like the other girls—the scowlers and the talkers—I am last in line, and I have to wait until all of them go through the course. Every girl goes down the slope, and each time the coach has comments about turning or edging. I can't even think. I have to pee so badly, and time is crawling. Finally, it's my turn to go. I take off, and seconds later I feel warm liquid running down my leg. I'm not even sure at first what I'm feeling. I'm just trying to see the gates and not get in trouble for my lack of concentration or my poor edging. But then I feel more of it. I am peeing, and the inside of my pants are soaked. I am terrified everyone can see from the back, and I'm sure that everyone is already laughing. At the bottom of the hill, I get my bindings undone and run for the chalet bathroom. Kelly sees me and I'm sure she knows, and I rush into a stall, sopping wet and mortified. Tears pour down my face as I sit there in complete silence. What will I do? Maybe I'll die in the stall.

After a long time, Mrs. Sherntanner comes in. She has another new baby—there are so many that I've lost track—and she starts nursing in the stall next to mine. After a few minutes of wondering if she's the right person to talk to, I decide she is and say hello. She tells me to come and look at her new baby. I love babies. They are soft and loveable. I know that one day I will have a baby and love her like no one has ever loved a baby before. Mrs. Sherntanner's baby has tiny hands that are squeezing together and pushing on Mrs. S's skin to make the milk come out faster. "Does it hurt?" I ask. Mrs. S. laughs and gives me her little baby girl to hold. At this point, I have forgotten about the peeing, and I can only gawk at the tiny baby in my arms.

After five minutes with the baby, I'm calm enough to ask Mrs. S. if she'll call my mom. "I have a better idea," she says. "I'll take you home. I want to say hi to your mom anyway." On the way to my house, Mrs. S. doesn't say a word about my accident. She talks about her babies, and I ask her why she has so many, and she says that she loves to have them. "Also," she says, "we're Catholic, and we believe in having large families." I decide that I won't tell my mom this. She has problems with Catholics already—she has problems with anyone who is different than we are—and I don't want to give her more reasons. But my mom is happy to see Mrs. S. and her baby. She holds the baby, and who wraps its fist around her finger. The day ends much better than it began.

things to think about

1. Some adults just know how to be with kids . . . they don't
    have to talk about it and that's a way to talk about it.

2. Being the best isn't necessarily the same thing as being
    the best competitor.

3. Babies have the power to make grumpy people happy
    because they love you no matter what. Dogs are that
    way too.

9.
my paris fairytale

Fifth grade is like fourth grade all over again. It's all about hair—I have Ms. Haire again, and the year starts with a focus on my own hair.

My sisters have tons of stuff in the bathroom—products for their eyes, faces, lips, fingernails—all kinds of stinky and interesting stuff that you see on TV. There's a foam that you can rub on your legs, and it takes off all the hair. Why would anyone want to do that? I barely have any to start with.

One day after cleaning out my closet and organizing my drawers again, I go into the bathroom, which is messy. Margot likes to yell if she sees me, but sometimes there's a tube or bottle just sitting there begging to be looked at. Today it's a bottle of Sun-In, which is a special spray that makes your hair blond, like it was kissed by the sun. The commercial shows girls walking around on the beach and there's a song that sounds like Bobby Hebb's "Sunny." I love the sun. I love kisses. I love beaches and I even like the Bobby Hebb song. It all seems like a fantastic idea.

I read the directions and spray my hair, but after watching my head in the mirror for a few minutes, nothing is happening. I spray again and again and again. Still nothing. Oh, well. I go to swim in the river and then lie on the deck with Mommy by the Olympic pool while she uses a huge reflector for tanning. I sit as long as possible and then hop up to play with Kitsy and Mr. Bubba and jump on the trampoline.

The days go by like that, and then one day I notice that my hair is getting blonder. It is actually orangey. Is the Sun-In working? I love it. But then the next day it's a little more orange, and I start to think that maybe the extra squirts were a mistake. Yellow blond is fine. Orange blond, maybe a little less. Red blond? That's a bold look, especially for a girl about to go back to school. The first day, though, was like a club: lots of kids had weird-looking reddish-blond hair, all thanks to Sun-In. By the time school pictures are taken in late fall, my hair is more yellow again, but everything growing in is so dark that I look like a skunk or a bumblebee.

nine

TOWARD THE END OF THAT YEAR, our whole family goes to Europe. Muffet is already there, working with a French author and translating his novel into English. We start our trip in London doing all the things you do there: Big Ben, Piccadilly Circus, even the Tower of London, where all the royal jewels are kept. They are guarded by men who stand stock still no matter if you dance a jig, scream, make funny faces, or even fart. Those guards have to be the strongest men in the world not to react to anything. Thinking about them, I kind of know what it's like to see things and not react. That's kind of how I am in my own house.

Mommy let me get a peacoat before we left, and I am glad to have it. It's cold and wet, and my peacoat is cute and warm. Daddy, Margot, and I walk the streets while Mommy stays in the room and meets us for meals, tea, and shopping at Harrods. Harrods is the Biggest Store in the Whole World, with entire floors dedicated just to dolls or chocolates or even tea—kind of like a museum. I get to buy a dress for Sylvie, my baby doll, who was originally from Europe. I also get dress shoes like Dorothy's in *The Wizard of Oz*, not sparkly but red and gorgeous. I forgot to tell you that my hair is now short again. My mom said

my stripes were ugly, so she cut off the yellow parts herself. I thought it would be hard to feel like a girl again, but
maybe my hair will get longer in Europe.

THE BEST THING IN LONDON is our hotel, the Cado-
gan. We have such a pretty room, and every day we go
downstairs to high tea, which means pinkies and scones.
Even that can't compare to our next hotel, the Ritz in Paris.
Because my grandfather Ernest had spent time there, they
named the bar and a lot of drinks there after him. At the
Ritz, we're treated like royalty. It is the most special place
I have ever been. Everything is gold: the bathroom fau-
cets, the lights, the picture frames, and even the chairs.
My parents get a huge suite, and Margot and I share a
room attached to it. Oh my goodness, could life get any
better than this? The Ritz staff wakes us up in the morning and opens our curtains like we live there, and then
they bring warm croissants and coffee with milk. I feel like
a princess—until Margot decides that she is the princess
and I am the maid, which doesn't bother me because Cin-
derella was a maid too. Take that, Big Pants. That's what

we call Margot behind her back because she always wears big pants and worries about getting a little fat. It isn't very nice, but sometimes she isn't very nice. Still, she's my sister, and I need to try to be good to her. She can be really funny when she wants to be, so I guess you have to see the nice in people whenever possible.

MARGOT AND I FIGHT LESS, and she fights less with Muffet too. Muffet shows Margot her neighborhood, introduces her to her boss, Paul Bonnecarrère, and takes her to all the places she goes to hang out with artists and writers. Muffet wears scarves and flowy skirts, which make her look artistic. Margot tries to dress the same way, but she just ends up looking like a wild cowgirl. Daddy takes me out every day and gives me a book, *A Moveable Feast,* which my grandfather wrote about his time in Paris with my grandmother Hadley. Daddy asks me to read the book so that I know about the places before we get there. I'm a slow reader, but being in the places where my dad lived as a baby makes reading easier. We go to the apartment where my grandparents first lived, and to the zoo where my grandmother took my dad when Ernest needed quiet, and to the train station where my grandmother lost my grandfather's writing. We go to restaurants where my dad is treated like a celebrity. Even just walking through the Tuileries Garden is special. Daddy tells me that his dad sometimes rode with him in his bike basket through the gardens to the Louvre, the most amazing, huge, super exhausting museum in the world. There's a painting of pears by a man named Cézanne, and Daddy shows me this painting and tells me how his dad wanted to write the way that Cézanne painted pears. The pears are simple and look like pears, but not like pears in a photograph. My grandfather wanted to write in the same way, to understand things from the inside out and make them both different than real life and more like real life than real life itself. It was a painting but you could smell and taste the pears just by looking at them. It's hard to explain, but if you saw them you would understand.

After Paris, we stay in a French village called Perouges. No cars are allowed into the place at all, so it seems like a village from a long time ago. It is stormy and cold, and our rooms are like a dollhouse castle, with little fireplaces and high beds with steps leading up to them, white canopies, tons of pillows, and fluffy comforters. Even though it is cold outside and walking is chilly, it's amazing when you come back in and they have hot chocolate with real milk already made and waiting for you. Being at Perouges is like being in a fairy tale. My parents fight, but not as much as at home. Muffet comes with us, and we're amazed that we can order whatever we want from room service. One morning, a woman opens the shutters and brings us crois-sants, just like at the Ritz, and Margot and I laugh at how many we can stuff into our mouths. I manage about four. She gets in four, maybe five. I run to Mommy and Daddy's room to show them, and when I get back to the room I see Margot sticking her finger down her throat and throwing up the croissants. I don't tell her I'm there because I know that it's something she shouldn't be doing. It feels awful and wrong, and it scares me. I start to shake. Why would anyone *want* to throw up, especially something that had been so much fun to eat? I never will understand it, but this wasn't the first time I saw Margot eat and get sick. It's just another thing that makes me feel bad, but I think it makes her feel even worse.

things to think about

1. God created croissants for you to eat when He wants you to wake up happy.

2. Nicknames are nice when you can say them to people's faces, but they're mean when you can only say them behind a person's back.

3. I always worry about what people think of me. I should be careful what I think and especially what I say about others.

4. If you think good things about people, they can be good, and if you keep thinking good things about yourself, you can be good too.

5. It's good to see where your parents came from because it's where you came from too.

6. Sometimes people feel bad after they eat, even though eating made them feel good at the time.

10.
horses are wiser than people

Mommy doesn't really like skiing. She only skis once a year, and this year the mountain she picks is Baldy. She takes her first run on College, the easiest run, and after a few turns she crosses in front of a beginner skier, who smashes into her and then takes off. Mommy is bony, and she practically breaks into a million pieces. The biggest bone in her leg is broken as well as two bones in her ankle. I want her to come to my race, but she isn't going to make it. In fact, there will be no more skiing for her ever again. From that dark January day on, Mommy stays in bed with her leg propped up and a cast from the tip of her toes to her sharp hipbone. It is a huge white cast that she lets us draw on for months—I was even allowed to write my name and hearts on it. One day, maybe because of the pain pills she's taking, Mommy even lets us paint her cast. Margot makes a self-portrait she says is like a Picasso; to me, it only looks like a person with too many heads.

Once Mommy stops taking her pain pills, though, the fun is over. She's grumpy, itchy, and unable to move. I clean her room and the kitchen, and I make all the beds every day instead of just once in a while. Many nights, I sleep in the bed with her because my father has moved down into the basement. All winter, I help, and it's tiring. One night, in the middle of the night, Mommy nudges at me until I'm awake enough to get the cat, who is throwing up a mouse at the window of her bedroom deck. Gross. But I do it. I hold her arm while she limps to the toilet, and I sit in the closet until she's done. Sometimes I wish Daddy would come back upstairs so I could sleep until morning, but I would never leave Mommy. She is beautiful and sad, and I love her. She cries even more now. I feel sorry for her.

After four months, Mommy's big cast comes off, and she gets a little one just above her ankle. This is easier. She can get downstairs with her crutches, and she even makes dinner some nights. Daddy buys a leather lounge chair that reclines, and she can sit in it with her legs outstretched and watch TV and eat dinner on a tray. This is when we quit eating dinner together at the dinner table. It isn't comfortable eating at the table anymore anyway, so we eat fancy gourmet meals on trays after Wine Time and no one says anything.

ten

I HAVE TAKEN UP horseback riding with my new best
friend, Sara. She has a horse called Revel (or Chocolate
Revel, after the ice cream). We always ride bareback, and
summer on a horse is better than anything ever. We ad-
venture all around the valley on trails, or we swim in the
river on the horses. I am obsessed. This is the summer
before sixth grade and after the very challenging Year of
the Broken Leg. Things seem to be going better on that
front. Mommy limps but has no more cast, and she's back
to tending the garden and being unhappy with Daddy and
everyone else except me. I still sleep with her, of course,
but without those middle-of-the-night disruptions. And it's
summer, which is a magical time.

My aim is to show my mom and dad that I should be
able to have my own horse because I am the most responsible person in the whole world. When I am not with Sara
and Revel/Chocolate Revel—I ride a horse borrowed from
the Sun Valley Center—I am at the stables in Sun Valley mucking the barn, feeding and grooming the horses.
There is something about horses that makes them amazing

to spend time with. They know that you love them. They look at you with their dark brown eyes and seem to say thank you. They talk to you all day long if you know how to listen—a glance, ears pinned back from anger or attentiveness, a nudge into the stall corner when you are trying to get them saddled. Sometimes they just want you to leave them alone for a minute. I take care of the horses that belong to the rich people who live in Sun Valley. They can afford to have someone else take care of their horses, and they only come once a day and ride with fancy English saddles, doing dressage and jumping. It's fun to watch, but it's not the kind of riding that I like. I like riding without a saddle and running through fields and rivers.

I also have a job guiding trail rides for tourists. Tourists can be the most annoying people on earth. They always say they can ride, but then they get on a horse and they're scared to death—and the horse knows it. Someone kicking the stuffing out of a horse is a sure sign they have no idea what a horse likes. Horses can also tell if someone is nervous, and they let you know. When I get a nervous tourist, I have to act very serious and tell them there must be something wrong with the horse they're on so they don't feel bad. Some people have to be taken back to the barn and given a Pokey Joe horse, which they should've had in the first place. Usually I do the easy thing—pair an easy horse with an untrained rider. Every once and a while, though, there's a dad who gets cocky and insists that he can ride. I realize there's no arguing with him, so I give him a horse that can run, knowing that I'll eventually see the horse bolting for the barn and the dad holding on for dear life. Those guys tip the best because they don't want their wives to know how silly they were out there on the trail.

I work hard that summer. Every day I tell my parents how much responsibility I have at the barn. There's a problem, though, which is Margot. She was allowed to have a horse two years earlier, and she wasn't responsible. The horse jumped the fence daily, and she could never get him off the highway by herself. He liked to buck, and in the end Margot was too afraid to ride him. "Who ended up taking care of it?" Mommy asks, meaning herself, and she's right. She ran after him in the middle of the cars in her skirt and sun hat. But I want a horse so badly. I can feel his withers under my legs when I'm sleeping. Mommy and Daddy never see things my way, though. They just tell me to keep riding at the Sun Valley Center and playing with Sara in the river, and soon summer will be over and the horses will move south for the winter anyway. I don't understand parents sometimes.

things to think about

1. *If you want to know what freedom feels like, go swimming on a horse.*

2. *Horses are wiser than people—especially tourists.*

3. *Being the hardest worker doesn't guarantee success in getting what you want from your parents. Your sister (or brother) might mess up before you, and you end up getting punished for it. Life, it turns out, is not always fair.*

11.
losing mr. bubba

I have two best friends. First, there is Kelly, the same one from the movies at the Sun Valley Opera House. She is the friend I can be silliest with. We have a radio show. It's called the Kelly & Mariel Radio Hour, and it's full of talking, songs, and mostly jokes. We do everything: the music, the interviews, speaking in foreign accents. I am best at French, and Kelly is great at a Mexican Frito Bandito accent like the ads on TV. The biggest part of the show is the Hour of Laughter, which is just an hour of us laughing until we're sick from it. I love being at Kelly's house, even though they keep their Christmas tree up past April. Everyone there smiles all the time. Jack, Kelly's dad, acts gruff but isn't really, and he teases me a lot but never hurts my feelings. Marylou, Kelly's mom, is the most smiley person ever. She smiles as much as my mom frowns. I don't remember her ever getting mad at us. She loves to plan trips in their camper. Sometimes Kelly and her family go all the way to Mexico. I can't get over that. I can't imagine my family in one car together for longer than a trip to town for groceries or maybe a dinner party in Hailey. When we go anywhere real, it's separately: Dad and me fishing in Oregon, or Mommy and me meeting her friends in California and going to Disneyland and Sea World.

Kelly is my best human friend, but my other friend is Mr. Bubba, my yellow lab. He has big ears and too-big feet because he hasn't grown into himself yet. All summer he plays with us and stays with me, riding, climbing, swimming, and living the good life. One Saturday, I wake up early and let Mr. Bubba out for his usual morning romp in the garden. Sometimes he goes to the neighbors' porch for a snack of bacon that Mommy won't let him have at home. I decide I'm going to ride my bike in to Ketchum early. I get it ready, but I have to say good-bye to Mr. Bubba first and let him know I'll see him later when Daddy brings him to the river. He isn't around, so I call his name over toward the neighbors' house, which is pretty far away, at least an acre or so. I call and call. I make sure he isn't in the backyard making a mess of Mommy's lettuce or petunias or simply biting at butterflies in the wind. After I search the backyard, I ride out to the highway. He's not supposed to go there, and he knows that, but there have been a few times when he's explored over that way.

eleven

"Mr. Bubba!" I call. "Bubba! Come here, sweet Bubba!" I go up and down the highway repeating my call. I go north because that's where we walk sometimes, and I know where Bubba likes to play. There's a drainpipe he likes to sniff around in, and I hear scuffling when I get close to it. It echoes in there, and I hear rumbling. I rush inside it. At the far end, I see a heap of yellow fur, and there he is, my Bubba, breathing too hard and trying to kick into the air to make himself stand. His breathing sounds wet and labored. He's been hit by a car, and no one even stopped. I pick him up. He is nearly the same size that I am. I run down the road toward our driveway, Mr. Bubba's long legs dragging on the ground. He's bleeding all over my new yellow smocked shirt. "Please, Bubba," I say. "Be okay. Daddy and I will take you to the vet. Hold on, Bubba boy. You're okay, Bubba, you're okay, my Bubba boy. You are sweet and tough and good." I don't know how I make it to our driveway. It's far, and Bubba is heavy. I scream for someone to come outside, fearing that if I leave him he'll disappear. Daddy comes out in his tennis shorts. He has no shirt on. He lifts Bubba right into the backseat of our Peugeot, motions me in, and then hops into the driver's seat.

I don't know if they make Kleenex boxes big enough to hold all my tears. I can't see for the fog in my eyes. I'm not crying out loud, just talking to my Bubba boy and telling him he's okay. My eyes betray me, though. "His breathing is getting harder, Daddy," I say. "He's still bleeding. Lots of it."

"It's okay, Mariel," he says, but his tires tear up the highway, and I know that he doesn't think it's okay. Mr. Bubba was hit hard, and blood is coming from his side and out of his mouth. He looks at me with a scared side-glance. I know he's hurting, and I want to make it better. He loves me. He says so. I know he wants me not to be mad at him. He thinks he did something wrong.

"I think the blood is choking him, Daddy."

"Mom called the vet. They'll be ready when we get there."

The vet's office is past Ketchum, so Daddy drives straight through all the lights in town without a thought. I love my dad in times like these, but I wish there were never times like these. I can feel Mr. Bubba slipping away. "Daddy," I say, and this time he doesn't answer, just tightens his jaw and drives a little faster. At the vet, a nurse wearing a pink dress over pants with paw prints all over them is standing outside. She runs to the door and takes Mr. Bubba. I want to go in, I want to see him get better.

eleven

Daddy says the vet is the best around and that he'll do everything he can.

We wait in the parking lot silently watching the sky and listening to the cars pass by on the road. Hawks circle the field across the street, and the crows above them, waiting for the prey left behind. Daddy does some squats and fake tennis swings into the air. He found clothes in his car, so now he's wearing a fishing vest. He looks silly. I get warmer and warmer in the sun. I am lying back on the roof of the car letting the heat burn into me. It's only fair that I feel as much pain as Bubba. Why did I let him out? Why didn't I go with him? Why didn't I pay attention? What did I do wrong? The vet comes out. He is bloody now too. He says Bubba fought hard but that his cuts on the inside bled too much and he didn't make it. He died on the operating table. My voice is faint and faraway: "Please, can we take him home to bury him?" The lady in pink says he's at the back door. When I go to him, he's still warm, but now he feels harder to my touch. When a living thing is so good and never unkind, why is it taken? Why do we have to feel so bad? I never want another Saturday like this in my life. I throw away my new yellow shirt, which has flowers on it. I wanted it so badly. I wish I had never wanted it.

things to think about

1. God makes you lose the things you love most so that you can feel the pain that others feel every day. Is that why horrible things happen? It is the only reason I can think of.

2. Losing your best friend hurts more than any hurt you can feel.

3. Even the biggest pain you can ever feel lessens over time, but you never forget how much you loved.

4. I want Mr. Bubba back, and I wonder if he will show up one day as someone or something else. Another puppy, maybe.

12.
what if my mommy dies?

Sixth grade marks the end of my easy days. It starts well. I'm still shy, but I get by, do good work, do the right things at home. Kids sometimes still whisper "rich bitch" because they think that I own the school, but most of that has stopped, and I feel more and more like myself.

In the fall, the ski team does dry land training, which means running up hills in the cold, and when I go up hills into the dark, it's really hard. The other girls are just like they are during ski season—competitive to an extreme. They sprint and try to beat each other, acting like they're just casually jogging as they spring past you, laughing. I can keep going, but I can't keep up. When my mommy and daddy made me, they didn't make me for speed. So when I have to push myself hard and fast, I feel like I'm going to bust open. I don't like dry land training because it takes the fun out of being outside, and you can't enjoy where you are. Whenever I go out and climb by myself, I feel strong and powerful. It's the same at school or on the team: I feel one way inside myself, but I act another. If my head and body could sync up, that'd be a miracle. Maybe I'm just not meant to do things with other people. My best times always happen when I'm alone.

This is also the year Daddy and some other parents and friends decide they want to start a school of their own. They've had a lot of dinner parties with various parents, lots of Wine Time with ideas from everyone, and they've all decided that the high school isn't a good place anymore. It's all the way down in Hailey, and the teaching is "crap." That's what Daddy says, at least. Margot couldn't learn there, and when Muffet was there she was bored. Out of these complaints, a new school is born. At first it seems like the greatest thing in the world. What could be better than having a school where your dad is a teacher? That's right: my dad is the French and Spanish teacher because he speaks both fluently. He plans to teach the first year, and then they'll find a real teacher.

Technically, I still have my last year at Hemingway Grade School, but I want to go to the new place, even if it means skipping a year. Daddy says it would be better to stay at Hemingway, but I know I'll never ever get a chance to have my dad teach me again. He asks all the other parents/teachers/wine drinkers if I can go, and because there are only thirty-five students—not to mention the fact that when the adults came over for dinner I did my best at serving them wine and food—they can't say no.

The school is in a church basement, which has a great feeling of ritual. I wouldn't say God is there because I don't think that way about God. But it feels special to be there, and making cookies for morning break is fun when it's your turn. But when it comes to classes, I start to feel lost. I hate to admit it, but jumping ahead of myself was a mistake. I do okay with French, of course, but when it comes to geography, geometry, and algebra, everything gets jumbled in my brain. All the angles, the Latin, and the sentence diagramming whirl around in my head. Daddy, as smart as he is, can't help with anything but French. One of the other founders, Julie, is our English teacher, and she seems to think it's perfectly reasonable to give out 50 to 100 pages of reading a night. I start to feel like I'm drowning, but I can't let anyone know because I don't want to appear a failure. Every night after dry land training, exhausted, I look at my homework in a sad panic. What did I get myself into? Most nights I can't even really stay awake.

Ski team goes okay. After dry land training, I am racing well. I win in time trials and get pretty close to winning some races, though the pressure of races, the idea of competition, turns me inside out. It's weird to take the chairlift up with girls who pretend to be my friends when really they want to beat me to a pulp. I usually come in fourth of fifth in a race, which isn't horrible but never great. The only good thing about races is that sometimes Daddy will drive me and my friends to locations away from home, places like Jackson Hole, Pocatello, or Driggs, Idaho. I love when Daddy drives. He speeds like a wild man, and we shriek with delight. We sing, we whistle, and we eat Hostess stuff from the gas station. Daddy and I go to fancy restaurants for dinner, eat big steaks and baked potatoes with all the fixings while the other kids have to go to Pizza Hut or McDonald's. I have never eaten at Pizza Hut or McDonald's ever, and all the kids think that's weird. Sometimes, when Daddy can't drive us, he gives me enough money to go to a nice restaurant by myself. I like that because the waitresses are always nice to me. They think it's cute that I'm there by myself and offer me free desserts if I want them. Of course I want them.

twelve

OVER SPRING BREAK, I go with Kelly to San Onofre, California. The plan is to spend every day on the beach, playing and cooking out and getting as tan as coconuts. We drive all the way there from Ketchum, and it's the biggest blast ever. Their camper is fully equipped with beds, a kitchen, toilet, and even a shower. Also, I'm allowed to bring whatever food I like— pasta, cucumbers, and my mom's home-baked bread. We buy huge blocks of cheese for the endless quesadillas Kelly and I plan on eating every day. My fear of getting sick is still with me, but I know that bread and quesadillas are safe for my stomach. What isn't safe is shrimp and fish, which they have at almost every roadside stand on the coast, and which Kelly's dad loves to order. I shake my head and say no thank you when he offers me some. Those things can sometime give you food poisoning, and you could throw up for hours and hours after that. Seafood: not for me.

It's a great vacation, though I'm worried about nights. Sleepovers are not my favorite thing, with my blankie and stomach medicine hidden in my pillowcase. But Kelly notices my blankie one of the first nights and says that it's cool and never laughs at me about it when I tuck it around my pillow. We sleep outside, on the roof of the camper, literally under the stars. When I'm scared or lonely, I take my blankie in the quiet night and rub my upper lip on the silk until I fall asleep looking up at the sparkly sky. I pray to God to protect me, to keep me healthy and happy throughout the trip, and I wake up every morning okay.

Spring break is three weeks long, so San Onofre is like a mini summer. Every morning, Kelly's dad drives the camper the short way from the parking lot down to the beach before dawn, so when Kelly and I wake up, we're already there. We go down the ladder to the crashing waves and come back for breakfast right there on the beach. They sometimes have sausage, but I stick to Life cereal, the one Mikey eats, with milk and bananas. Then it's out to the water for body surfing. I'm bad at it at first. The ocean scares me. Even the small waves seem like they're out to get me. But Kelly's dad makes me go out, even when I get tossed around inside a wave. He wades out toward me, barking orders that I can't really hear, but having a dad-type person barking orders is comforting. Over that first week, I get good enough to feel like I'm not failing at something, and toward the beginning of the second week it occurs to me that I might even be succeeding.

This is also the first year I start to feel pretty, or at least somewhat. Kelly helped me pick out a new bikini before we left Idaho, and out here on the beach, with my tan and my longish hair with real blond in it, I notice boys looking over our way. Some of them are looking at Kelly, which makes sense: she's a year older and has boobs already. But some of them are definitely looking at me. During the first weekend of the trip, we're lying out on our towels when some local surfer boys come by to say hello. Kelly flirts with one of them, who has blond hair, blue eyes, and skin as dark as someone from an island. He has a friend, and I try some flirting too, unsure of what that involves exactly, apart from wearing a bikini, giggling just enough, and acting slightly uninterested. "I hope you come back next year," he says. I think what he means is that he hopes he sees me when I'm Kelly's age, with boobs, and I agree.

One afternoon, we spend the morning with our surfers, running on the beach and laughing. Kelly's boy tries to teach me to throw a Frisbee. I'm good at it pretty fast, and my boy notices and says something nice. When the two of them finally take off for home, Kelly and I are so tired that we flop down on our towels and let the sun bake our backs. All of a sudden, it's a little cooler. I turn onto my side. Kelly's parents are there, standing over us, blocking the sun. They don't look happy. "What?" Kelly asks. But they are looking at me. "What?" I ask.

"You have to leave," Kelly's father says. I'm panicked. What did I do wrong? Are they mad about the surfer boy? Do they think something happened that didn't happen? There wasn't kissing or anything like that, and I don't even think that I had many impure thoughts about him, at least until he said nice things about the way I threw the Frisbee.

"It's your mom," he says. Now I'm panicked all over again. What happened to my mom? "She's in a hospital," he says. From there, I see his mouth moving, and details appear in my mind, but I'm not sure that I'm actually hearing him. She's not in Idaho but in Portland, near where Mary Kay and Dan live. The reason is her broken leg, sort of: she had been feeling weak ever since the accident, and Daddy decided to take her to the doctor to make sure there wasn't something more seriously wrong with her. Kelly's dad has an expression on his face like he knows more than he's saying.

Daddy has arranged for me to fly to Portland. Instead of a big jet like we took to Europe, I get on the smallest plane I have ever seen. Two men I don't know are the

twelve

pilots, and my spring break disappears into a bumpy ride up the West Coast. The whole thing feels like a chairlift in a windstorm. I breathe slowly through my nose, taking little sips of air when my tummy turns over inside me.

It's raining in Oregon. Daddy meets the plane, drives to the hospital, and then stops the car in the cold parking lot. "Let me tell you what's happening," he says. He starts to talk, then stops. "Are you cold?" he asks me. He wraps his jacket around me and says we need to go upstairs. His voice is thick, as if there's something stuck in it.

Dan is up there in an empty room with a couch, a bedroom dresser, and a Mr. Coffee machine. Daddy seems calmer with Dan there, and he starts to talk again. When the doctors looked at Mommy's leg, they found that she was sick with something else, and they had to knock her out to cut into her throat and take out a blob called a tumor. "So they took it out?" I ask. He shakes his head. When they got there, they found that it was too hard to take out without hurting her more. Instead, they sewed her back up again and decided that they needed to think of a different way of making the tumor go away. Daddy is having trouble talking again. "The doctors don't know what they can do, really," he said.

"What do you mean?" I say. I don't understand at all.

"They're worried that Mommy might not live very long," he says. I stare at him. He's wearing a khaki fishing shirt. Dan is too, along with pants bunched up at the bottom. It hits me like a punch in the stomach. They've gone fishing. While Mommy is flat in the bed with doctors worried out of their mind—"they don't know what they can do for her, really"—Daddy and Dan went fishing. I am disgusted with both of them. "Let me see her now," I say. My voice sounds older, harder. They lead me down the hallway, which smells like the senior home my grandmother lived in when she got old. I look down at my still sandy flip-flops, which squeak against the floor as I pass endless closed doors with handles bigger than my arms. My feet are freezing. The cold and rain from outside feels like it's seeping in to me.

Daddy and Dan, the two stupid fishermen, lead me into Mommy's room. At the last minute, Daddy interlaces my fingers in his. I look at him standing there in his jacket, three times my size. His face is creased like he's in pain. I forgive him for fishing. That's what he does when he gets sad or scared. He walks me closer to the bed. Mommy looks beautiful lying there. She's completely still.

twelve

A mask for air is on her chest. I notice Mary Kay on the
other side of the bed. "Puck," she says. "Marielzy is here."
My mother's eyes flutter open. She says hi. She calls me
"baby girl." She holds out her bony hand, nails glisten-
ing with shimmery pink polish. The hospital band is too
loose around her wrist. I take her hand in both of mine.
"You look pretty, Mommy," I say. "You don't look sick at all.
You did your hair." How can I explain how much I love my
mommy in this moment? Mommy is being her kindest self,
which is easy to love. She pulls me close to her and puts
her cool hand on my cheek. "You can't die, Mommy," I say.
"I love you, and I'll make sure you live. I promise, I'll pray
harder than any person could ever pray, and then you have
to stay here. You have to. And you have to have to promise
me you'll pray too...."

My mother looks at my hair. "You're blonder," she says,
and then she laughs too loud, like we're watching a TV
show and something funny has happened on-screen. I'm
scared that she's laughing this way, and I start to cry. She
wipes my lashes dry and holds me. "Okay," she says. "I will
be okay for you." I ask her to promise, and she does. Then
I put my head on her tummy, scared to get too close to her
throat. Her chest rises and falls with her breathing, and

I watch the raindrops through the wires in the window screen.

We stay in Oregon with Dan and Mary Kay for a week. I sleep alone in the attic and ignore the dolls at night. Every day we make the long drive from Salem to Portland Hospital. Mommy gets stronger, and Daddy has meetings with the doctors to decide what to do when we get home. She will start something called chemotherapy and radiation in Boise. That will attack her tumor. Daddy will drive her, and when he can't, I will. He's already taught me to drive because I had to make trips to the market when Mommy had her broken leg the year before. I've been driving without a license since last year.

106

things to think about

1. Parents have a hard time talking about what hurts. They try all kinds of ways to make it okay.

2. Flying can take you from a place in the sun to place in the rain in a very short time.

3. "Tumor" is a word I don't like to see, hear, or think about.

4. When you drive without a license, you have to be extra careful. You or your dad could go to jail if you get caught. That's what I was told, anyway.

5. Cancer might be something that happens when sadness can't get out of your heart.

13.

listening is the best way to show you care

The next months are my time for helping. I learned that when Daddy was sick, and I learn it again with Mommy. When you have a sick parent, you have to say yes, even when you're not sure what yes means. Sometimes yes means getting up in the middle of the night to make sure Mommy can make it to the toilet to get sick. Sometimes it means letting Kitsy in to prevent hours of meows. Sometimes it's as quick as testing to see if Mommy's ginger ale is cold enough, and sometimes it's as simple as sitting on the end of the bed while she tries to watch *Mission: Impossible*, her favorite show. And yes *always* means lots of patient smiling, as if you understand how hard it is to have cancer. That's the hardest yes because I know that I have no clue. Mommy is dizzy all the time and skinnier than she normally is, which means that there's always at risk of something bad happening.

It is incredibly hard, but I can't think of any alternative. I feel like being with her all the time, except when I'm at school. I put all my prayers into her, trying to make sure that God doesn't forget her while He is dealing with so many other people. I figure that if I keep focused and do everything that's asked of me, everything else will work out. After eight trips to Boise, Mommy isn't doing well, but she isn't doing as badly as they thought she might. I'm not sure how much I helped, but I didn't hurt.

Here's one thing we do together: Mommy thinks that I'm talented at entertaining, so whenever we watch TV together, she asks me to sing and dance for her. I imitate the commercials, sort of like I did with Kelly on our radio show. The Serta Perfect Sleeper ad with Joey Heatherton is her favorite. I pretend I'm Joey, dancing and singing with my fake microphone all around her bed, leaping onto the chaise lounge, lying in a sexy pose on the edge of the covers, all the while giving Mommy googly eyes that I think are sexy. She can't stop laughing. And the more she laughs, the more I swing and lunge across the room, singing the mattress song until we both dissolve into hysterics. I love to laugh, and getting my mom to laugh is the best thing ever.

Here's another thing: Mommy has no more hair, so she wears silk scarves like a French artist—or at least that's what Muffet says on the phone. Mommy's skinny face makes her teeth look big. I do her makeup and make sure the edges are even, even though she says if she can't see the lines of base on her chin then no one else can either. That doesn't work for me. I don't want people to come over and see her white neck and a slightly beige bronze face that ends at the jawbone. I smooth her lines and apply her lipstick, every once in a while testing the peachy glaze on my own lips. She is much healthier looking when I'm done and happier to be seen with her "face on."

We cook too. I learn how to broil lamb chops, make scalloped potatoes, and fry liver with onions, which I eat even though liver was never my best friend. I plug my nose on those nights, but Mommy loves it. Maybe she needs it. Here is my theory on food: I think that if you eat good food—not fancy food but good food like vegetables, salad, liver, and even fish and potatoes all from places you know, whether farms of forests close to where you live—it makes you feel better just like medicine would. I can't figure out why people don't make their diet part of their treatment when they're sick. Even when I think of Margot or Muffet and how kind of crazy they sometimes get, I think that maybe if they didn't drink wine or eat too much dessert or things that look unhealthy to me, like white foods, they would be calmer. This is when I decide to get really careful with what I eat. I try to make Mommy eat only things that seem good, healthy, and kind to her tummy. I make her eat healthy brown toast and jam made from only berries, and then I make her eat wild and brown rice and things that aren't complicated. Nothing comes out of a box. I tell Daddy that her food has to be simple, even when he makes complicated dishes for himself. Mainly I make it so that our food is always full of colors. If Daddy catches fish for us, I eat it without sauce, just straight from the grill with butter, salt, and pepper. I eat broccoli and baked potatoes and sweet potatoes, and I tell my dad I'm not sure if eating margarine is good for us anymore.

I start reading all the labels on our food, and if the ingredients are long and foreign to me, that food doesn't pass inspection. We stop buying Carnation Instant Breakfast and cheese in a can, which is sad because it's fun. No more sugary cereal or yummy crackers like Ritz or Wheat Thins, even though the woman who advertises Wheat Thins was a gymnast and it's hard to say no to her. I tell my mom these preservatives aren't good for her cancer, and she rolls her eyes. But she lets me do the grocery shopping and feed her most days anyway. I learn how to make black beans and rice, a tomatoey beef dish over rice, and also macaroni and cheese with a real cream sauce. When she's having a strong day, I help her make whole wheat bread, and we eat it hot together with honey and French butter. I make fried chicken in a skillet and it's delicious, but the frying seems unhealthy, so I learn how to make it in our oven by coating it in flour made from nuts. The first time I try it, it comes out dry and gross, but then I rub the chicken legs and thighs with butter and coat them in the nutty flour, and it's great. The bad batch goes to the neighbor's dogs. Cooking makes helping fun and makes saying yes easier.

It's a different summer. Instead of spending whole days in town, I stick close to home. I jump on the trampoline a lot and look for anyone who will watch me. I can do front flips and backflips and layouts and a million add-ons. Sara and Kelly come over sometimes, but everyone and everything is quieter. I save a robin whose nest has fallen, and watch her eggs hatch. I watch a beaver make a dam, and I name the fox that's stalking our cat Snifty. I really miss town outings, but I ride my bike up to Galena Lodge, almost twenty miles north, at least three times a week. On the way home, I sometimes go to the hot pool at Easley

Creek. It's a church camp, full of all kinds of kids from big cities who are bored with the mountains at first, but by the end of vacation they never want to leave. I watch them try to jump into the river for the first time. They certainly don't like cold water like I do, but they do it anyway. I usually can't stay long enough to get to know them well, but it's enough time for them to ask why I'm able to ride so far away from home by myself.

SOON AFTER MOMMY GETS SICK, Margot goes to work for someone who has something to do with Evel Knievel, a guy who has a crazy plan to jump across the Snake River in Twin Falls. Evel Knievel tries jumps like this often, sometimes on a motorcycle, sometimes in a rocket car. He's a total nut job. People call him a "daredevil" as if that's a real job or something. Margot is hired to help convince people to come see him, though I'm not sure that Evel Knievel needs much help getting people to come see him. While she's there working with Evel Knievel, someone tells her that she's beautiful, which she quickly tells us. I'm not sure why she tells us. Does she want us to say that she's beautiful too? I think she is, in many ways, but she's also my sister, and I don't know if I think of her in that way.

After he tries his jump, Margot never comes home. She says something about going off with the people she met, and then something else about New York City. The next thing you know, Daddy and I are at Atkinson's Market and guess who is on the cover of a fashion magazine. Margot, our very own Big Pants! At first we think it's someone who looks like her because the woman on the cover is blond, but her name is right there. Well, sort of: now it's spelled Margaux, like the wine Chateau Margaux. In an interview in another magazine, my sister says that's the story behind how she was born, that Mommy and Daddy were drunk and in love when they made her. It's half-right at most. But that's her story, and she more she tells it the more I have to get used to the fact that Margaux is the same as Margot but also different. Margot was the one who was in the house with me, making mean expressions or telling me what to do. Margaux is the one who goes places to be pho-tographed, who is paid insane amounts of money to wear fancy clothes by fancy designers. Soon Margaux is one of the biggest models in the world. She's even on the cover of *Time* magazine.

It's strange but still kind of neat at the same time. The next time I see her, it's Christmas, and she gets off the plane in Hailey looking like a star. She's nicer too— she comes toward me and hugs me and kisses me on the cheek like I'm someone she's happy to see. "This is Errol," she says, pushing forward a man with a black mustache wearing a white suit and shoes. When Errol is far enough away, Mommy leans in to Daddy and says he's greasy, and Daddy tightens his mouth a little because he doesn't like saying mean things about people. But he does ask Errol where someone gets clothes like that. "It's not exactly winter wear in the mountains," he says.

The nicer Margaux asks me questions about school and friends and how things are going, and I answer her in a voice that I don't quite recognize as my own. Is this what happens when someone gets famous? Is it because she's getting attention? Is it because she's in love? She and Errol have lots of Christmas presents for us, and she talks about how excited she is to put them under the tree. On Christmas morning, she's up early, her eyes bright, sitting in the room by the tree. One by one, we tear paper and open boxes, and there's lots of smiling and hugging. I notice that Margaux's presents don't really make sense. Daddy gets a pink cashmere scarf that doesn't go with any of his khaki or brown pants, shirts, or jackets. Mommy gets a big box of nail polishes in dark colors, even though she only wears light pink or coral. Muffet gets tiny bottles of perfume almost like the alcohol bottles my parents get on the plane. I get a dress and a sweater that is clearly someone else's size. I wonder if they're presents that Margaux got because she's a famous model now—people are always giving presents to famous models. No one cares, though, because she seems happy to be giving them.

$$* \quad * \quad *$$

CAN HAVING A FAMOUS SISTER rub off on you? I spend lots of time thinking about that. A few girls in school know that Margaux is on the cover of magazines, and they congratulate me as if I had something to do with it. A few boys look at me a little differently. But there's no direct effect on me until Margaux calls my parents and tells them that she's been offered a role in a movie. It's called *Lipstick*, and she's playing a supermodel. "You should be able to do that without much problem," my mother says, and I can't tell if she's making a joke or criticizing Margaux or just being proud. But the news about the movie is only the beginning. My mother passes the phone to me. Margaux tells me that there's a part in *Lipstick* for a little sister, and she asks me to be in it with her.

I don't know what to say. I don't really understand what it means to be in a movie. I've only watched them, and not very closely—mostly I've been in the Sun Valley Opera House, dreaming of a boy holding my hand or staring at an empty seat worrying why the boy whose hand I want to hold is late. I've never thought about movies as things that are made. Daddy says it might be fun to go to New York and try out for it, and even Mommy says it sounds exciting. I know she wishes she could come. She's done with the chemotherapy and radiation, but she's still fragile. I stand near her bed and ask her again what she thinks, just to watch her get excited about the idea all over again.

Daddy and I fly to New York first class. I have never done anything this fancy. The seat is as wide as Daddy's leather chair in the living room. In New York, we go to a tall building, which is our hotel. It's not a normal hotel, though. It's the Plaza, which is where Eloise, one of my favorite book characters, lives. I look for her in the lobby even though I know she's not real. Then Daddy and I walk across a big park to another big building. There are so many people in New York, and they all seem to be on the sidewalk. At the second building, we take an elevator to the top floor and step out into a huge room with a swimming pool. A swimming pool all the way up here in the sky? It seems impossible. Margaux is there already, sitting on one of the pool chairs. Two people step out of a corner of the room and introduce themselves as the director (an older man about my father's size) and the producer (an even older man who is as short as a ten-year-old child). They say something exciting: "We want you to go into this swimming pool." Then they say something silly: "We want to see how you are playing sisters." I laugh a little bit at this. How can we be anything but good at playing sisters? We get into the pool, and mostly we just splash around in the pool and giggle.

After the scene in the pool, we stand in the huge room on the top floor of the big building and look at all the skyscrapers in the city, which are like a cross between needles and mountains. They are so tall, and they have so many people in them. I start to get a little dizzy thinking about them all. Daddy shakes hands with the director and the producer and asks me if I'd like to go to FAO

Schwarz. I nod because I can barely speak. It's like a city of toys, with dollhouses as big as any I have ever seen, and so many stuffed animals and toy cars and games. I find one dollhouse that reminds me of our house in California, and I bend down to look closely at the bedroom that reminds me of the bedroom I had when I was a little girl. Is there a tiny Mariel in there? What is she doing? Is she lying on her bed looking at the shadows on the ceiling? Is her sister tossing and turning noisily in the bed next to her? Are her parents downstairs fighting? I wonder if the tiny Mariel knows that in just a few years she will move to Idaho, where her grandfather was from, and that she'll get tall, and that her dad will get sick and then her mom will too, and then she will get taller, sometimes feeling lonely, sometimes feeling happy, and then her sister will ask her to be in a movie, and she'll come to New York and see a dollhouse with a tiny version of herself in it. It all makes me lightheaded.

Before we leave New York City, we have a private meeting with the producer. Daddy and I walk back across the park, this time stopping to look at the statues of characters from *Alice in Wonderland*. In a building next to the park that's even taller than the one with the swimming pool, we ride the elevator to the top floor, and a secretary takes us inside an apartment to an office with the biggest desk I've ever seen. The producer is at the very end of that desk, and he looks like a little kid driving a car. He's smaller than me, and his head is tremendous. Daddy says that men like him, powerful and rich men, like big things because they make them feel big too. Daddy likes him, though, and so do I, though I can't really understand him. He speaks with a very musical Italian accent and keeps kissing the air with his hands. I think he's saying he wants to make me a star along with my sister. Daddy agrees, and they drink a toast to all of it. I keep smiling, saying thank you when it feels like I should, and watch the pigeons flutter against the windows.

IT SEEMS LIKE A DREAM, and the dream continues: Mommy tells me that she's taking me to Los Angeles to make the movie. It will be sunny there because it's always sunny, and Mommy can go to stores that she can't go to in Ketchum and buy clothes for herself and feel better.

We stay with Daddy's fishing friend Stephanie. She's

called Big Stephanie, and her daughter, who is in college, is Little Stephanie. Her husband is named Efrem, but we never see him. Big Stephanie is lonely like Mommy and Daddy, and she drinks lots of wine because of it. I like Big Stephanie, partly because she's lonely. For most of my life in Ketchum, I've been to people's houses who seem happy and in love, with lots of smiling and laughing. Big Stephanie is nice, but she's also more alone than those people, so she's easier for me to relate to. Big Stephanie drinks and fishes like Daddy, and I think maybe Efrem feels somehow disappointed with the way his life has gone, like Mommy. Little Stephanie has a beautiful room with a wall of ribbons for winning first prize at horse shows. She has long, thick, brown hair and is very ladylike. I am fascinated by her. I wonder if she has to take care of her parents the way I do, and if she feels invisible sometimes.

Their place is enormous, with lots of land, buildings, and animals. It doesn't feel like there's a city nearby at all. We stay in the guesthouse, which has horses right outside the window and peacocks walking around on the lawn. The driveway is long and sloped and perfect for learning skateboarding, which is what I do when I'm not making the movie. We have a little kitchen of our own to cook in if we want to, but we usually eat dinner with Big Stephanie.

I go to the movie set a few days a week. Movies are like towns, and this one seems almost as big as Ketchum. There are people who only work with clothes and ones who only do makeup. There are people who bring you snacks, and they're different from the people who make you lunch. There are people who take care of watches, people who pull cables around, and people who pour glasses of water and wine (the wine is actually grape juice because you're never supposed to drink real wine while working). The strangest thing is that I don't have to do any of these things. I only have to do one thing, which is to show up and say my lines in a way that makes them feel real to everybody watching. Otherwise, I just stand still and people fix my hair or dress me. There's even a person to make sure that I look exactly the way I looked moments before, so when they start filming again a part of my clothes or hair won't jump from one place to another in the scene. They actually have to trim my hair once because of too much time passing in real life. We don't have bedrooms to go to during the day to rest. Instead, there are trailers with names written on them. Mommy and I are in a small one, and Margaux is in a big one. She has a TV, a bedroom, and a kitchen with lots of liquor bottles that are already open. It's a mess even though it's cleaned often. Mommy and I laugh because she's just the same here as she was at home. I wonder if Margaux is okay. She's not as mean to me, but I notice sometimes that she seems scared, as if she's not sure if she's where she's supposed to be.

The plot of the movie is complicated. In it, I'm a kid, and I introduce my teacher, who is played by a guy named Chris, to my sister, who is played by my sister. He likes her and attacks her. Actually, he rapes her, but that's not a word I like or even completely understand. My sister (in the movie) goes to court to try to get him put in jail. I make friends with Chris, who plays the bad guy, and with Anne, who plays Margaux's lawyer. She asks me questions in the courtroom scene, just like Perry Mason. I know that the questions are supposed to be hard for me to answer, and they are. When I look worried, Anne tells me to listen to her, and whatever she says I should answer with my lines in a way that comes from my heart. It makes sense. When I'm on the stand, I'm supposed to cry, and I do. I try hard to control my tears, but at the same time I know that it's the right thing for the scene, so I let it happen. When I'm done I feel good, like I did something real in a fake world.

Another day, we're filming a creepy chase scene at the Pacific Design Center, a huge building that isn't finished yet. It has a million floors and dark corridors where I have to run from the bad guy. Even though the scene is scary, running around the building is fun. I sometimes hang out with the girls who are in that scene with me, and one of them drinks carrot juice, which looks healthy. I ask if I can get some for Mommy and me, and sure enough the next day we have some too. Mommy won't drink it. She says I'm getting a little crazy with the health food.

I turn fourteen while making the movie, and get a surprise birthday cake on set. I have new school clothes and some wardrobe from the movie to take home. The whole crew loves Mommy. They make her feel like royalty. She loves them back, loves the attention and the distraction. For a little while, she forgets about being sick, and I forget about her being sick too.

things to think about

1. *I think acting is just being yourself with different clothes.*

2. *Acting feels like life without the forever.*

3. *Even in the city, you can find things to do outside that make you feel close to yourself.*

4. *Listening is the best way to show you care and the best way to love. Turns out it also makes you a better actor.*

5. *You have to be careful when you get lots of attention not to let it go to your head. You should always be polite and kind. Like Mommy says, "Pretty is as pretty does."*

14.
the winter goes away

When we get home from *Lipstick*, we drive to
Boise for a checkup to see if Mommy is getting better.
Daddy tells me that the doctors are hoping she's in remission, which would mean that the cancer is gone or at least
not spreading. But there's not remission. Instead, there's
new cancer in her spine. I feel horrible because I think it
might be my fault that it's come back. I didn't focus these
past few months. I got lost in the excitement of the movie.
Even though we had a good time, Mommy needed me to
concentrate on her cancer and making it go away. I tell
her that I'll pay attention so she can get better again. I ask
Daddy if they can make the chemotherapy less strong so
Mommy doesn't get as sick at night, and he says he's not
sure. So I ask her doctors, who say they'll do what they
can.

Mommy tells me that she's prepared to go through
whatever is necessary, and I see that she's determined, but
I see something else too, which is that she's lost most of the
happiness she had in California. I make a list of TV times

so that we can watch all the comedies she likes, and another list of foods that will help her get healthy. Daddy is being his best self and really helping. He makes the drives to Boise for her treatments while I go to school. "We're all in it together," he says, and I know what he means. One day, out by Watercress Lake, I tell him I think it's my fault she got sick again. "That's silly," he says. "The opposite is true. Mommy is alive because you love her so much." I feel like I can breathe again after he says that.

It's a nervous two months. Daddy takes care of Mommy during the day and I take care of her at night, and we get through it with Mommy dry-heaving sometimes and unable to sleep other times. She loses the little bit of hair that was coming back, but she has a whole new set of scarves that Margot sent her from Italy. School is still a struggle, especially as fall turns into winter. I try waking up at 4:30 in the morning, hoping that the quiet will help me absorb more of the reading. I don't get much done, but I really like that time of day, when the world is quiet except for animals and wind and water. Later on in the day, I have to deal with other people, and one of those people is my teacher, who never has anything good to say about my papers or grades. But what are papers, anyway? They are ways of preparing yourself for thinking about life, and I'm already thinking about life all the time. What I'm doing for Mommy seems important, and sometimes papers seem less important. And then there is a week where the work gets a little easier, and the teacher is a little nicer, and I feel less worried.

Time passes. The winter goes away, and Mommy's cancer goes away too. Summer is usually a happy time, but this summer feels a little sad too. Mommy is weaker and older. She can't do the things she used to do. It's hard for her to get around the house, and some days she mostly stays in bed. Still, she manages to make dinner and plant petunias a few at a time. I ask if she wants my help. "No," she says. "I love my purple petunias, and no one plants them right. You can go into town." As I take off on my bike, she yells after me: "Don't ride home uphill! It's too hard!" She knows I will, whether it's hard or not. As I ride away, I see that she is putting her hands into the dirt, and I know how good it must feel for her to be outside in the sun. I meet up with my friend Sara, and we ride and hang out by the river, eating Grape Nuts with apple juice because we've decided that milk isn't good for us.

At night, I lie in bed, looking at the shadows, the same

way I did when I was little. But I don't see the same things in them that I used to, even if they are the same exact shadows. Muffet is out of the house, trying to make sense of her life, even though making sense is the one thing that she can't exactly do. Margaux is out of the house, being famous, though she's starting to do more acting along with modeling, and I'm not sure how she feels about that. And I'm still at home, still a kid, still helping out with everything and wondering if there will ever be a time when I'm not a kid. What's past being a kid? Being a grown-up? It used to seem impossible, but now I'm not sure. I did a photo shoot (like Margaux) for *Seventeen* magazine, which is cool. Kids in town still call me Mertz, Stretch, or Spider, but I feel different. Life is changing, and it's changing me. My hair is past my shoulders now, and I'm tan, and even though I still have no boobs, I'm growing up, literally getting taller by the day.

I see a shadow shape that looks like a ramp, but I'm not sure if it's going up or down. Life mostly seems to be uphill. It's hard sometimes, but that's all right. I don't mind that part of the ride. Part of life is learning which things you can't change and which things you don't have to change. I know that my parents don't get along like other people's parents do, and they probably never will. That makes me sad, but I also know that they have a different kind of love for each other that's strong in its own way. I know that Muffet will never be normal, but she will always be beautiful. I know that Margaux will always want more attention, more love, more food and drink, more everything because something inside of her feels empty. I love her too, and I hope that the day will come when we're comfortable with each other. I know that Daddy is smart and kind and feels confused and lost at home but peaceful when he hears a river, a stream, or the flush of birds. I know that Mommy is sick and will probably be sick for a long time, but at least she's alive; she promised me she would fight to stay in the world, and I believe her. I know that even though she seems unkind, there's a part of her heart that is funny and sweet and warm with love. No one can see that because she doesn't show it to anyone. In some ways, my mom is as invisible as I am. When I watch her, I see her wishing she wasn't mad at everything and everyone.

The shapes in the shadows on the ceiling don't tell me everything. The are shapes I don't completely understand, mysteries, questions that I want to answer. But

I have started to understand that I don't have to answer them all at once. I'm getting sleepy. I push myself flat into the bed. Are there problems? There are always problems. But they're not what's pushing me flat into the bed. I'm doing that, because I want to see things a certain way, and maybe I don't want to always be seen. And when I'm down there, flat against the bed, I feel a calmness wash over me. My life is good, and maybe always was, and I'm not sure I want anything more than summer, icy water, Alice Lake, and horseback riding through the grass. I have my family, which isn't perfect, and Idaho, which is, and I am okay.

where to go for help

Childhood is a strange time. It can seem as if the world is filled with pitfalls and perils, and that there's no way to fix things.

This is especially true when it comes to mental health and family health issues. There are so many difficulties that families deal with, and some of them can create a vicious cycle in which trying to deal with them creates even more problems. And kids are in a tricky position. They feel powerless, but they're also right at the center of the story.

That's why I think it is so important to give you a list of organizations to contact for help. No matter what your problem is, it isn't only your problem. Families have troubles because they are made up of people, and people are complicated. My parents drank wine all the time, and that led to me feeling like I wasn't really getting all of their attention all the time or in the right way. And that in turn made me the kind of person who always tried to control the environment around her. My sister Muffet had problems with mental health, and my parents didn't always

135

know how to deal with her, which not only complicated her care and treatment but affected the rest of us.

In those days, fewer people went for help because people didn't really knew where to go for it. There were organizations like Alcoholics Anonymous, certainly, but people were more likely to keep their problems inside. I didn't even really talk to my friends about my family—not in that way. Partly it was because of shame and frustration, but it was also because my vocabulary for discussing those kinds of problems wasn't completely worked out yet. That meant that I wasn't having open conversations about alcohol, or mental illness, or my mother's cancer, or my own issues with food. If I had had access to those resources, everything would have been different. I'm not naïve enough to think that counsel, advice, and empathetic talk would have solved the problems completely, but they would have made me feel differently about them.

The list below should help you at least get started in figuring out where to go if you have problems that you feel are too big or too scary to deal with alone. Maybe your mother is taking too many prescription medications and it's starting to affect the way she acts. Maybe your father is starting to spend too much time alone, and when he does join the rest of the family, he has a violent temper. Maybe you are secretly throwing up the food that you're eating. Maybe you're taking drugs and find yourself slipping into an place where you can't take a measure of your own self-control. Or maybe it's not even anything that dramatic. Maybe it's just a sense that something unhealthy is eating away at the core of your family.

Again, kids are in a strange position. You don't pay taxes. You don't work at an office. Some of you don't drive. So why should you have to deal with any of this? Remember: being a kid isn't the same as being powerless. You have the same access to the telephone as anyone. You can call the same hotlines as anyone. If you think there's something that serious that you need to deal with, start the process. Kids are sometimes the most observant members of families because they aren't loaded down with all the baggage that comes from being an adult. They might not have the experience and wisdom to know how to fix problems, but they're fully aware of them.

Good luck with whatever you're dealing with, and never be afraid to ask for help.

ALCOHOL

THOUGH I AM NOT AN ALCOHOLIC, I spent my whole childhood watching my parents drink—sometimes socially, sometimes more problematically—and over the course of my life, I have known many people with alcohol issues. It's so common that sometimes it's a blind spot in American culture. I'm always moved when I hear stories from friends who have dedicated themselves to the 12-step program or found a truer sense of self by attending daily meetings. Above all, these programs help launch people on a journey to understanding themselves.

Alcoholics Anonymous

aa.org

212-870-3400

Adult Children of Alcoholics

adultchildren.org

562-595-7831

Al-Anon Family Groups

al-anon.alateen.org

757-563-1600

DRUGS

Each new generation of kids fights its own battles against drugs—not only the kinds of drugs, but the way that drug use unfolds against the broader social background. I myself have lived drug free, for the most part, but I've observed the destructive effects of drugs on people close to me, including my sisters, and I see more and more how society struggles with legal drugs too: prescription medications are more of an issue than ever before, for both kids and grown-ups. Like alcohol programs, organizations dealing with drug addiction promote mindful and conscious living.

Narcotics Anonymous

na.org

818-773-9999

MENTAL HEALTH

WHAT IS MENTAL HEALTH? More important, what is general mental health? I tend to think that it's a category made up of many smaller categories: if you're struggling with seeing the world clearly, or with seeing it with balance, perspective, good humor, and flexibility, there's usually some other more specific underlying cause. But if life seems overwhelming, you have to start somewhere, and general mental health resources can help lead you down the road to awareness and recovery. I am very connected with the following organizations: I've spoken to groups under the auspices of NAMI and McLean Hospital (where I am an honorary board member), and I try to embrace any and all organizations that promote help and understanding. Again, don't be afraid to make more than one call if one doesn't seem like enough. Your needs (or the needs of your mom and dad or your siblings) may be served better by one organization than another, or by a combination of them.

National Alliance on Mental Illness (NAMI)
nami.org
800-950-6264

National Institute of Mental Health
nimh.nih.gov
866-615-6464

where to go for help

McLean Hospital

www.mcleanhospital.org

800-333 0338

Substance Abuse and Mental Health Services Administration

findtreatment.samhsa.gov

877-SAMHSA-7

OBSESSIVE COMPULSIVE DISORDER

I PERFORMED OBSESSIVE BEHAVIORS throughout my childhood. I was surrounded by so much chaos, and I wanted so much for the world to be orderly. That was fine until I started to feel like those behaviors were controlling me. Obsessive Compulsive Disorder (OCD) is a mental illness that needs to be treated.

International OCD Foundation

iocdf.org

617-973-5801

DEPRESSION AND MOOD DISORDERS

DEPRESSION IS MORE COMMON than anyone realizes, even among children. What your parents think is normal moodiness might be something more persistent—something that's being caused by emotional issues or even environmental factors (diet, physical illness, and so on). It's also one of the most commonly ignored problems, not just by others but by depressed people themselves—there's shame associated with it, and also a sense of helplessness that often prevents people from seeking assistance. Whether you're dealing with a depressed parent or grandparent or feeling depressed yourself, these organizations offer compassion and purpose to help you deal with it.

Anxiety and Depression Association of America
adaa.org
240-485-1001

Depression and Bipolar Support Alliance
dbsalliance.org
800-826-3632

Families for Depression Awareness
familyaware.org
781-890-0220

SUICIDE

HAVE YOU EVER KNOWN SOMEONE who has committed suicide? Have you struggled with suicidal thoughts yourself? Suicide is one of the hardest things to understand. Why would a person want to leave the world? What I have learned from watching my own family and listening to the stories of others is that there isn't just one kind of suicidal thought or action. Often, there is no clear line dividing suicidal impulses from intentionally failed attempts from successful attempts. A suicide can be planned carefully in advance or can be the result of one difficult day or traumatic incident. I have worked with organizations to prevent suicide because my grandfather and sister took their lives (along with other relatives), and I want people to know as much as possible about the signs and what they can do to prevent this mental illness. It's preventable if we all talk about what we are afraid of and what we think we can't talk about—that's one reason I wrote this book. I have assisted in the efforts of the American Foundation for Suicide Prevention, but all of these groups do their best both to help people with suicidal thoughts and to support families that have lost their loved ones. If you are at all worried, even for a minute, that you are heading down this path, don't hesitate to call.

American Foundation for Suicide Prevention
afsp.org
800-273-8255

American Association of Suicidology
suicidology.org
800-273-8255

Suicide Prevention Resource Center
sprc.org
800-273-8255

National Suicide Prevention Lifeline
suicidepreventionlifeline.org
1-800-273-TALK (8255)

Suicide Awareness Voices of Education (SAVE)
save.org
952-946-7998

CANCER

Illnesses are a difficult topic for kids. Most kids are healthy, but at some point, too, most kids have to deal with the presence of illness in their family. I learned that early on: my mother was diagnosed with cancer before I was a teenager, and I spent twenty years watching her dealing with it and dealing with it myself. Later, when I was married, it happened all over again with my husband. I have seen people endure dealing with cancer, and I know that a life lived with cancer isn't only about medicine. It's also about mental health, exercise, diet, and the way that the disease is discussed. These organizations can help.

American Cancer Society

cancer.org

800-227-2345

CancerCare

cancercare.org

800-813-4673

Cancer Support Community

cancersupportcommunity.org

888-793-9355

Burzynski Clinic Advanced Alternative Cancer Treatment

burzynskiclinic.com

713-335-5697

Caregiver Action Network

caregiveraction.org

202-772-5050

DOMESTIC VIOLENCE

KIDS WHO GROW UP in violent homes are much more likely to suffer from mental and emotional issues later on. Combining the intimacy of family life with the destructive patterns of abuse makes for incredibly toxic situations. For all those reasons, these are some of the most important resources for kids. If you see a parent or loved one being abused, or if you are being abused yourself, take steps immediately to get help. Don't hide what's happening out of shame or fear. All those things just perpetuate the problem. Grown-ups who are in abusive situations need help dealing with them just as much as you do, so any steps you take are good ones, even if they might not seem like it at the time.

where to go for help

The National Domestic Violence Hotline
thehotline.org
800-799-7233

Children's Safety Network
childrenssafetynetwork.org

FOOD AND EATING DISORDERS

EVERYONE EATS, but not everyone eats healthfully. My own obsession with food began in childhood and lasted for many decades. And these days, I see so many children—mostly girls, but boys too—who struggle with food and body image issues. People worry that they're too fat and cut back on calories without thinking about how it will it affect the rest of their development. People exercise too much and become preoccupied with the changes in their bodies years before they're done growing. If I had known of organizations like this, I would have dealt with things earlier and in a healthier manner.

National Eating Disorders Association
nationaleatingdisorders.org
800-931-2237

Overeaters Anonymous

oa.org

505-891-2664

To every one of you:
"You are not invisible. I see you,
I hear you, I believe in you."